C000157897

WELWYN GARDEN CITY PAST

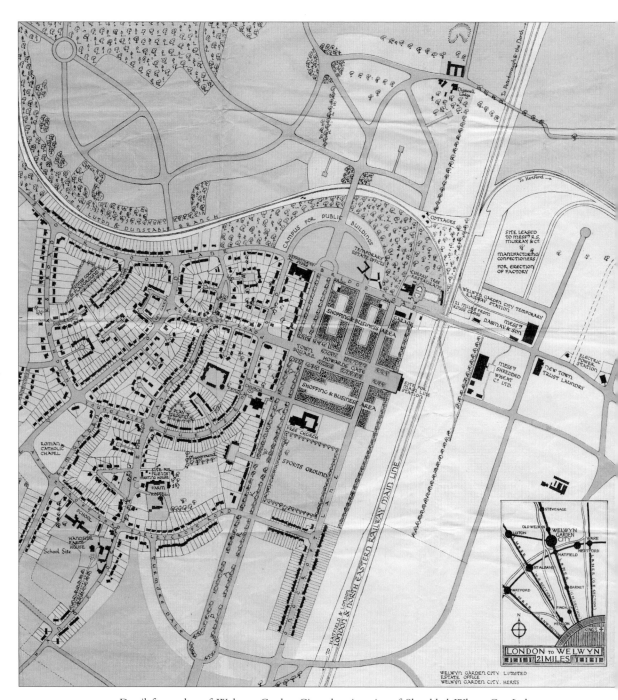

Detail from plan of Welwyn Garden City, showing site of Shredded Wheat Co. Ltd.

WELWYN GARDEN CITY PAST

Tony Rook

Best wishes

Tony Rook

Christmas 2001

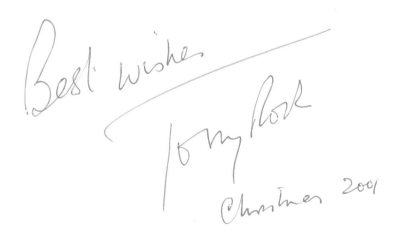

Phillimore

2001

Published by
PHILLIMORE & CO. LTD.
Shopwyke Manor Barn, Chichester, West Sussex

© Tony Rook, 2001

ISBN 1 86077 141 6

Printed and bound in Great Britain by
BIDDLES LTD.
Guildford, Surrey

Contents

List of Illustrations vii

Acknowledgements ix

Preface x

1. Ebenezer Howard 1

2. The Land 6

3. Settlements 12

4. Churches, Fields, Farms and Inns 18

5. Country Seats 38

6. The Public Good 49

7. The Company 71

8. Town Structure 82

9. After the War 110

Bibliography 127

Index 129

List of Illustrations

Frontispiece: Detail from Garden City plan

1. A diagram from *Tomorrow* 1
2. The Panshanger Estate sale 2
3. Part of the 1898 one-inch Ordnance
    Survey map 3
4. The Digswell Park area *c.*1950. 4
5. Geological map of the region 6
6. Fossils found in the area 7
7. Road subsidence, 1979 8
8. Old Cottages in Black Fan valley 8
9. Lockleys Roman villa excavation, 1937 9
10. The old *Salisbury Arms* hotel, Fore Street . 10
11. A typical Cowper escutcheon 11
12. Neolithic axe-head from Danesbury 12
13. Bronze-Age arrowhead from Digswell 12
14. The 'Panshanger' Belgic chieftain's burial . 13
15. The sites of known Iron-Age and
    Roman settlement 13
16. The third-century Roman baths
    excavation at Welwyn, 1970. 14
17. Map showing Gill Hill 16
18. Domesday Survey entry for Welwyn 17
19. Map showing the creation of new parishes . 18
20. Saxon burials, The Grange, Welwyn 19
21. Watercolour of Welwyn church, 1832 . . . 19
22. The rear of Welwyn church 20
23. The church at Ayot St Peter 21
24. Aerial view of Hatfield House 22
25. Hatfield Market House 22
26. The Old Cottage, Bridge Road. 23
27. Digswell Lodge Farm. 24
28. Attimore Farm 24
29. The 1599 map of Digswell 25
30. Field boundaries as marked on the
    Tithe Apportionment maps, *c.*1840 26
31. 1796 map showing strip fields 27
32. Houses at Hatfield Hyde 28
33. Map showing the various farms in the area . 28
34. Stanborough Farmhouse. 29
35. Welwyn village from the south, 1967 29
36. An aerial photograph of Welwyn village . . 30
37. Welwyn High Street, 1902 30
38. Commercial premises in Welwyn village . . 31

39. Advertisement for the land sale
    at Hatfield Newtown, 1848 31
40. The original Salisbury Square 32
41. A late 19th-century view of Arm and
    Sword Yard, Hatfield 32
42. Commercial premises in Hatfield 33
43. Wrestlers' Bridge, Hatfield 33
44. Postcard view of Hatfield 34
45. The minute book of the
    Welwyn Turnpike Trust. 35
46. The old turnpike-keeper's cottage 36
47. The *Salisbury Temperance Hotel* 37
48. 19th-century painting of Panshanger House 38
49. Detail of the 1599 Digswell map 39
50. Old cottages at Digswell Water 40
51. Digswell House in use as an army hospital 40
52. Lady de la Rue at Lockleys, 1917 41
53. Brocket Hall by John Charnock, 1780 . . . 41
54. Joseph Sabine and his family 42
55. The original design for
    Tewin Water House 43
56. An early engraving of Hatfield House 44
57. An early plan of Hatfield Palace 45
58. An interior view of Woodhall, 1831 45
59. Ludwick Hall. 46
60. Map of Tewin Water, 1797 47
61. Digswell Mill before restoration 49
62. Mew's Brewery *c.*1920. 50
63. Hatfield Brewery 50
64. A steam-driven brewer's dray 50
65. The *Red Lion*, Digswell Hill 51
66. Church House, Welwyn 52
67. The first Garden City police station, 1936. 52
68. A glass gaming piece 53
69. An 18th-century playbill 54
70. Title page of the rule-book of the
    New Union Society 55
71. Dr. Edward Young's first school 55
72. The Last Day by Kate Rook. 56
73. Roman hematite amulet 57
74. Certificate of 1683 allowing Ann Harper
    to be touched for the King's Evil. 58

75. An obsolete sewage pumping station 59
76. The Queen Victoria Memorial Hospital . . 60
77. Welwyn Vestry minutes 60
78. The disastrous fire at Danesbury, 1920 . . . 61
79. The old Fire Station, Hatfield 62
80. Park Street Baptist Chapel, Hatfield 63
81. St Mary Magdalene's, Hatfield Hyde, 1957 . 63
82. Detail from the Welwyn Tithe Map, 1837 64
83. The Great North Road 65
84. Digswell on the Great North Road, c.1904 65
85. Dugdale's map of c.1840 66
86. Welwyn Viaduct, 1850 66
87. Blow's beehive works, c.1898 67
88. Lord Salisbury's private waiting room 67
89. Ordnance Survey map of
      Welwyn Garden City, 1898 68
90. Early Garden City railway station 68
91. Welwyn Garden City railway station
      before its official opening, 1926 69
92. The rail crash in Welwyn tunnel, 1866 . . . 70
93. Sketch map of the Garden City 71
94. F. Osborn and T. Chambers on the
      newly purchased site, 1919 72
95. The book produced by the
      New Towns Trust 72
96. The Company's Electricity works 73
97. One of the Company's steam waggons . . . 74
98. The west front of the Company's laundry . 74
99. Stanborough Farm 75
100. Woodhall Lodge Farm 75
101. Brickwall Farm house 76
102. Molly Jenkins with her caravan 76
103. Nos 34-8 Parkway during construction . . . 77
104. Creation of the Rural District of
      Welwyn Garden City, 1927 78
105. 'Concrete' houses being built 78
106. Lower Handside Farm 79
107. The Garden City's first bank 80
108. Air-raid shelters being dug 81
109. Ordnance Survey map of the
      town centre, 1925 82
110. Workmen's huts, 1920 83
111. A brick kiln in Sherrards Wood 83
112. One of the Company's waggons 84
113. Light railways before the war 84
114. The light railway, c.1930 85
115. De Soissons' 1920 master plan 86
116. The town centre, 1959 87
117. A map showing the
      Garden City 'Lanes' 87
118. *Punch* cartoon of the Gum Boot Era 88

119. The first Welwyn Stores 88
120. Aerial view of Welwyn Stores 89
121. Howardsgate from Stonehills, 1966 90
122. Welwyn Stores, 1950 91
123. Posters advertising the healthy environment 92
124. Welwyn Garden City poster 92
125. The interior of Dawnay's steel works 93
126. Welgar Shredded Wheat factory, 1939 . . . 93
127. Subsidence in Broadwater Road, 1973 . . . 94
128. Murphy Radio factory, 1955 94
129. Welwyn Film Studios, 1928 95
130. The ICI site, 1976 96
131. Lincoln Electric's factory, 1960 96
132. The Barcley Corsets factory 97
133. The High School, Digswell Road 98
134. Heronswood School, 1958 99
135. The Grammar School, 1958 99
136. Peartree Farm maternity hospital 100
137. The Queen Elizabeth II Hospital 101
138. Ordnance Survey map of the
      town centre area, 1939 102
139. Friendship House, Tewin Road 103
140. The *Green Man* c.1930 104
141. The original *Cherry Tree* public house . . . 104
142. Welwyn Garden City swimming pool . . . 105
143. The Clock swimming pool 106
144. View over the new Chequers, 1959 107
145. Lawrence Hall 108
146. Electric milking at Upper Handside c.1920s 108
147. The Embassy Cinema and Theatre, 1981 109
148. The Pavilion Cinema, Welwyn 109
149. Demolition of Springfields' Phoenix
      'pre-fabs' 110
150. The *Welwyn Times* announces the
      purchase of Lockleys 111
151. The layout proposed by the Company . . 112
152. Hatfield Hyde 114
153. Welwyn Development Corporation's
      Master Plan of 1949 115
154. The development of Welwyn Garden City 116
155. The structure of Howardsgate Trust Ltd . 117
156. The Howard Centre, 1990 118
157. Coneydale after the bombing, 1940 119
158. Construction of Welwyn by-pass, 1926 . . 120
159. Accident on Welwyn by-pass, 1965 120
160. An experimental roundabout 121
161. The Campus from Welwyn Stores 121
162. The Campus car park, 1963 122
163. Sir Theodore's Way, 1959 122
164. Welwyn Garden City town centre 123

Acknowledgements

Perhaps this should be 'apologies'? So many people have been involved in the shaping of this work that I am sure my list is incomplete. I must thank the staff of organisations which include Hertfordshire Archives and Local Studies, Welwyn Garden City library, the Louis de Soissons Partnership, St Albans Diocesan Education Centre, Mill Green Museum, English Partnerships, J.M. Dent & Sons, the *Welwyn Times* and, of course, Phillimore & Co. Individuals worthy of thanks are Alan Adams, Geoffrey Beynon, Richard Busby, Peter Clayton, Chris Conway, John Dettmar, Derek Dewey-Leader, Angela Esserin, Henry Gray, Robin Harcourt-Williams, Marion Hill, Yolande Hudson, Ron Ingamells, Jim Macrae, David Milliner, Terry Mitchinson, R.H. Reiss, Marquess of Salisbury and Dennis Williams. Special thanks to A.C.J. Scott, a literate oldest inhabitant, and to my wife Merle, without whom I wouldn't, almost literally, get very far. As for surviving errors, the buck stops here.

I have used photographs, text and drawings from my own collection, other private collections, Hertfordshire Record Office (including those where copyright is owned by English Partnerships), Hertfordshire Local Studies Collection, and Welwyn Garden City library (including the *Welwyn Times* archive). It is often impossible to find the original source of photographs. Many identical pictures appear in several collections, both public and private, and are often second- or even third-generation copies. If anyone feels that I have infringed their copyright I apologise and should be glad to be told.

I should also like to know if I have mislabelled any photographs. The identification of archive pictures is often oral history and, accordingly, suspect. The item I have identified as Woodhall Lodge Farm (picture number 100), for example, I have seen in another collection labelled Digswell Lodge Farm, and at least three collections contain the same photograph (for obvious reasons I haven't used it) captioned Welwyn Garden City Gasworks. There was no gasworks in the Garden City.

Preface

This book is about a few square miles of rural Hertfordshire that changed the world. For centuries history passed them by along a road between two rural towns. For more than half a century others sped through, indifferent, on the railway. To them this was 'England meditative', where nothing happened, nothing changed. The landscape they saw from their carriage windows was the result of evolutionary processes; here people lived, played, loved, laboured and died.

Then one man had a vision of a town here, and set about its creation. Modern history has concluded that this was 'A Good Thing' and criticism seems tantamount to heresy. This is in part because existing accounts of its history were written by protagonists in the creation of the town, or people for whom it was cradle and patrimony. They saw its failures as glorious adventures, its faults as endearing. Culturally, though, the place is arid, and has never produced a concert hall, viable art gallery, museum, or professional theatre. Its early inhabitants therefore come over as health freaks, enthusiastically shouting, 'Come on in; the water's lovely!'

What was achieved here has shaped our ideas of town planning and our environment. A sincere idealist conceived a utopian Garden City, but we should not be blind to the fact that his conception was brought into the world by men whose competence and true motives we must deduce from the evidence of their activities.

One

Ebenezer Howard

Ebenezer Howard was born in 1850. His education was far from academic and he started work in 1865 as a clerk in the City of London, copying documents with a quill pen and becoming a self-taught stenographer. In 1871 he emigrated to the United States where, within one year, he failed as a farmer and became a shorthand writer in Chicago. He experimented with the design of typewriters, and thereafter attempted to produce a shorthand machine. He once said that he was an inventor, and that he invented the Garden City.

Returning to England in 1876, he worked as a stenographer, and for some time as a parliamentary reporter. In 1879 he married Elizabeth Bills and they had four children. She was a propagandist of his ideas and provided much-needed management of the family finances. She once wrote to him, 'I could wish that the good Lord who made you a Social reformer had also given you the wherewithal to reform on.'

He was a Congregationalist with a strong philanthropic faith, who once said, 'Religious and political questions too often divide us into hostile camps'. In the discussions of religion, science, economics, politics and sociology in his church and professional life, he would stand a little apart, but after consideration became a very persuasive speaker. At one time he was even a preacher.

Tomorrow

In 1888 he read a novel, *Looking Backward*, in which a modern Rip van Winkle wakes in A.D.2000 to an America run on co-operative, communistic principles. Influenced by its ideas, he published, in 1898, *Tomorrow: a Peaceful Path to Real Reform*, suggesting his solution to the depopulation of the countryside and the overcrowding of the towns: 'Town and

country must be married, and out of this joyous union will spring a new hope, a new life, a new civilisation.' New towns should be created on agricultural land. They would be ring-fenced, to include an agricultural belt, and be planned for a specific limited population. Industry and housing should grow together, so that people would work within walking distance of their homes.

He visualised the land owned and administered by a central council with powers very like those of the modern local authorities, which would control the number of retailers, including public houses, but

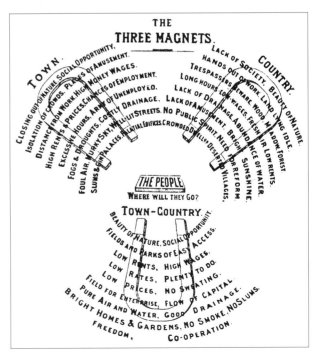

1 A diagram from *Tomorrow* showing the relative attractions of town, country, and town-country, of a Garden City.

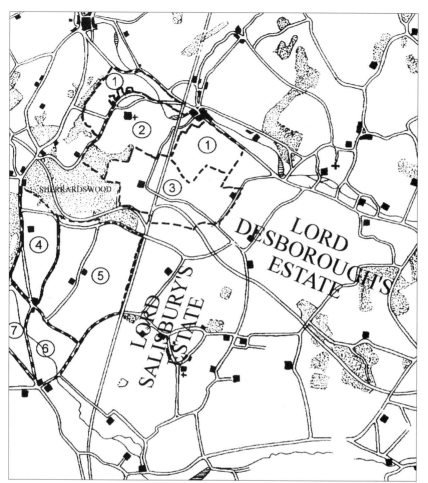

2 The Panshanger Estate sale. The lots bought by Howard are Digswell Water Farm (1), Digswell Park (2), Digswell Lodge Farm (3), Brickwall Farm (4) and Upper and Lower Handside Farms (5). The lots not bought by Howard are Stanborough Farm (6) and Roebuck Farm (7).

construction work would be undertaken by private enterprise or co-operatives. He included persuasive financial calculations. Trades unions and Friendly, Co-operative and Building Societies would be encouraged to provide loans for the purchase of houses. The increase in the value of agricultural land when turned into a town would benefit the town itself.

Idealised diagrams based on concentric circles illustrated the town-country concept. Activities would be zoned in order to ensure that everybody got the maximum benefit from the country and their proximity to employment, but would be spared the noise and pollution of the industrial areas. Around his Garden City were allotments and an agricultural belt.

Tomorrow was published in October 1898 and was both ridiculed and patronised by reviewers, but in June 1899 the Garden City Association was formed, dedicated to promoting its aims. In May 1900 it resolved to form a company: 'Garden City Limited'. Annual conferences were held in successive years at Bournville, where 300 delegates attended, and at Port Sunlight, where attendance exceeded a thousand. The venues were new towns created with, and for, industry by philanthropists, although their inhabitants had no choice of employer, and there was no agricultural element.

Letchworth

In 1902 the Garden City Pioneer Company was formed and Howard's book was reissued under the title *Garden Cities of Tomorrow*. In four months the share capital of £20,000 was fully subscribed. In 1903 the first Garden City Limited began work on

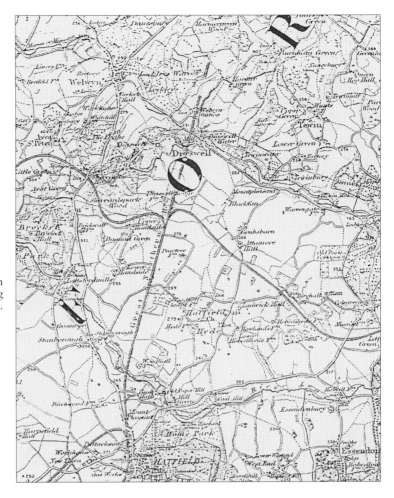

3 Part of the 1898 one-inch Ordnance Survey map showing the area covered by this book.

a site at Letchworth. Of the company's authorised capital of £300,000, £100,692 had been raised in the first year.

Howard and his ideas had achieved international recognition and many developments imitated Letchworth with 'garden villages' and 'garden suburbs', but these were commuter settlements which ignored the most important ideal, that of the self-contained town with integrated industry and agriculture.

Town Planning

The Association became the Garden City and Town Planning Association, which concerned itself mainly with the density and the pattern of residential development, and Howard formed the breakaway National Garden Cities Committee

with three colleagues. One was C.B. Purdom, who had come to Letchworth as an accountant and became an authority on garden cities. Frederic Osborn began work at Letchworth as the secretary and manager of the Howard Cottage Society. The third member was W.G. Taylor, of Dent & Co. Their publicity, especially a book called *The Garden City*, written by Purdom and published by Dent, changed the Association which the rebels rejoined. Purdom became its editor and secretary.

In 1919 Richard Reiss, barrister and lecturer, joined. He had published a book, *The Home I Want*, in 1918. The Rowntree Village Trust made a large donation to the Association on condition that he should become its chairman. By that time the population of Letchworth had passed 12,000.

4   The Digswell Park area from the north in about 1950. Digswell House is centre right and Welwyn by-pass top left. Monks School is now in the centre of the photograph.

The Association tried to persuade the government to sponsor more garden cities as the metropolis continued to grow. Without consulting his colleagues, the impatient Howard wrote on 30 April 1919 to the President of the Association, Lord Salisbury, asking if he would sell land north of Hatfield between the Lea and the Mimram for a second garden city. His lordship did not own all the land and did not wish his part to be developed. To a second letter, written on 4 May, Salisbury replied that he felt the utmost respect for the founder of the garden city movement, but he could only deal with responsible representatives of the Association!

The Purchase

Howard then learned that, by a remarkable coincidence, Lord Desborough intended to sell the west side of his Panshanger estate on 30 May. Although Osborn and Purdom believed it would weaken their case with the government if another garden city were begun by private enterprise, Howard himself set about borrowing money from friends. He told the auctioneers that he intended to bid for the land, but they did not inform Lord Desborough and recommended that Norman Savill, a partner in a firm of surveyors, should do the bidding on his behalf. He bought 1,458 acres for

£51,000. To round off the area Howard bought 230 acres of Sherrardspark Wood (excluding the timber) by private treaty shortly after. At the time George Bernard Shaw described Howard as an 'amazing man' who appeared 'an elderly nobody'. He was in his 70th year and had insufficient funds to pay for it all!

Historically the site was a backwater, separated from London by wooded land mainly unsuitable for agriculture, through which not even the Romans constructed a main road. At the beginning of the 20th century the area was entirely rural, with a few scattered cottages and farms and a population of about five hundred. The Great North Road passed it by. There was a railway junction – but no station – and, although there was a network of lanes, few of them were even metalled, let alone tarred.

What happened next completely changed the character both of the area occupied by the Garden City and of the surrounding district. This book attempts to outline, through a consideration of topics, the history of the region from just south of the River Lea to just north of the Mimram between Brocket Park and Panshanger Park, including Tewin, Welwyn (from which Welwyn Garden City somewhat confusingly took its name) and the old town of Hatfield.

Here, in a mere eighty years, has grown Welwyn Garden City, which now has a population of about fifty thousand. How did it all begin? Geological processes ultimately determined the development of the area, so the story begins a very long time ago.

Two

The Land

❖

Geology

The nature of a place and its people depends on what is beneath it. It was some sixty million years ago that a thick layer of chalk, a soft, white, calcium-rich rock, formed at the bottom of a warm sea. Later the chalk was covered with thin strata: 'tertiary beds' of acid gravels and clays. Tilted and elevated above sea level to form the Chilterns about thirty million years ago, the land could now be eroded by the weather. A large river – the Proto-Thames – flowed north-east across the region over the sites of the future Watford and Ware, and cut a valley between what were to become Hatfield and Welwyn Garden City. About 200,000 years ago a glacier covered the area. It blocked the valley, forming a lake over the sites of Watford and St Albans which eventually overflowed to the east, forming the present Thames valley. When the ice melted it left behind an untidy mass of material which it had carried: 'glacial gravel' and 'boulder clay'. These surface deposits were eroded.

Boulder clay is a heavy, sticky, grey clay which contains scattered stones of all sizes, hence the name. Exposed to the air it oxidises to a light brown. It includes a large amount of chalk, some in lumps, and therefore forms fertile soils. It was heavily forested, however, and largely uncultivated until the advent of heavy wheeled ploughs of the Saxon period. The tertiary deposits, clays and pebble gravels which form Sherrardspark Wood and the area south of Hatfield were too acidic to be used for arable land.

The River Lea, a tributary of the Thames, was 'captured' by the valley vacated by the Proto-Thames, and that is why it turns to flow north-east after it reaches Mill Green. Its valley contains gravels which are partly of glacial origin and partly left by the Proto-Thames. The Lea valley together with the younger Mimram valley delimit the plateau on which Welwyn Garden City came to be built. Relatively easy routes of communication were provided by the river valleys, especially the Mimram, as the chalk is exposed along their flanks for almost their entire length.

Swallow Holes

One phenomenon which was to have a considerable affect on modern construction in the Garden City, particularly in the north-east areas, is 'swallow

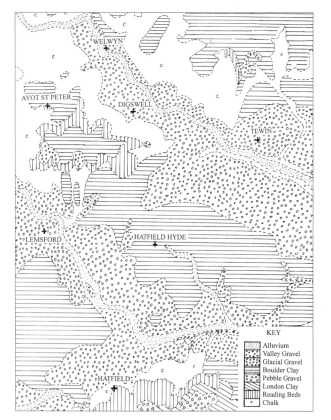

5   Geological map of the region.

6 Fossils found in the area. At the top are gryphaea ('devil's toe-nails') and belemnites from the boulder clay. Below are sponges, inoceramus (a shellfish) and sea urchins from the chalk and derived gravels.

holes'. Most of these are probably due to localised solution of the chalk underlying the later deposits by ground-water charged with dissolved carbon dioxide, which, under gravels covered by humus and vegetation, can reach levels almost one hundred times greater than that in rainwater. A fine example can be seen in Sherrardspark Wood, where water running off the clay capping disappears into a deep dell. More disturbing examples occur where gravel forming a dome bridging the hole suddenly collapses. Often the problem arises from the former practice of extracting chalk for liming the acid plough-soil from shafts opening out into large subterranean caverns. It is recorded that the shaft was then stopped

7 Road subsidence in 1979 in the aptly named Swallowfields area.

with brushwood and the soil ploughed back over the hole!

On the Panshanger development occurrence of swallow holes has led to the use of expensive

reinforced concrete foundations which project beyond the corners of the houses. A representative of the flying school, giving evidence in the hope of discouraging the proposed compulsory purchase of this land in 1948, warned that swallow holes frequently appeared there spontaneously.

Building Materials

Geology determined what materials were used for building. There is no hard local freestone so we do not know where early people lived, since most buildings were of wood, mud, thatch and the like, which do not survive. Labourers lived in hovels, traces of which are of no interest to, or have escaped the notice of, archaeologists.

Substantial vernacular buildings were constructed with timber frames. Some dating from the late 15th century survive, although usually greatly altered. The Old Rectory at Welwyn, for example, originally a moated manor house, has a fine closely-timbered frame with curved wind-braces, probably

8 Old Cottages in Black Fan valley before the Second World War.

9   The foundations of Lockleys Roman villa following the 1937 excavation.

reared in the late 15th century, but it has brick infill or lath-and-plaster replacing most of the original cob infill, and fine, large Georgian sash windows; none of the original internal walls remain. Church House is probably of the same date. Much of the timber frame of *The Wellington* is original. At Digswell Water a small row of timber-framed cottages has been much altered, and there are more timber-framed houses on Ayot Green. The timber frame of Ludwick Hall is probably of the 16th century, but with 18th-century additions.

Flint and Mortar

When burned, chalk turns into lime which, slaked with water and mixed with sand, gives a plastic mortar which sets slowly. The chalk also contains hard nodules of flint, which is brittle. The solid flint-and-mortar parts of Roman buildings have survived.

The Normans built their churches using coursed flint, with the quoins and reveals in 'clunch' or 'Totternhoe Stone', a soft freestone which was mined from the chalk outside our area.

10   The old *Salisbury Arms* hotel in Fore Street, Hatfield.

Brick

Once fired, clay hardens irreversibly to give pottery, brick or tile. The Romans produced thick
tiles, which they used with mortar in a way similar
to that of later brickwork, and thin tiles for
roofing. There was a Roman brick and tile factory
near Bulls Green. The first modern bricks were
imported from the Low Countries, but soon they
were being made locally. In 1470 the sum of
28s. 6d. was paid for carting 'tiles called brick'
from Hatfield to Bedwell; and the construction
of Hatfield Palace between 1480-90, it is said,
'marks the moment when brickwork became
fashionable in this country'. Queen Hoo is a fine
example of brickwork of about 1550. Hatfield

House, of 1607-12, made extensive use of the
new medium. While it was still expensive it was
left exposed for all to admire. Fine examples are
the early 18th-century Lockleys and the north
end of Welwyn mill-house. Buildings were even
covered by false brick casings, as at the *White
Hart* and The Grange, which was originally a
farmhouse, in Welwyn.

The most notable surviving part of old Hatfield
is Fore Street, described by Pevsner as 'A perfect
example of a self-respecting street in a small
Georgian town.' Apart from the old *Salisbury Arms*
(now the *Gate House*), however, the architecture
is illusory: many of the buildings are earlier, with
casings. Although many of the features are

genuine, they are the work of F.W. Speight, who tastefully improved them between 1910 and 1920.

There were brickworks either side of the Great North Road south of Ayot Green from the 18th century onwards, and individual estates had their own yards, the Cecils' (and later the Garden City's) being at Twentieth Mile Bridge and the Garden City's at Sherrardspark Wood. *Ad hoc* brickmaking also took place. The Great Northern Railway used bricks made locally from weathered boulder clay ('brick earth') for its bridges and the viaduct. The pits which provided this were between the railway and Longcroft Lane, and north of The Vineyard at the top of Knightsfield.

Stucco

After bricks became relatively cheap, the gentry often rendered them with lime-based stucco to produce houses that appeared to be of fine masonry. The false front of Guessens (another farmhouse) in Welwyn and Earl Cowper's surviving early 19th-century country houses in the Mimram valley, Digswell House and Tewin Water, are examples of the classical style of this period. At this time many timber-framed buildings were also hidden behind lath-and-plaster.

Roofing

Tiles started to replace thatch locally for roofing important buildings before 1200, and the Great Hall at Hatfield was re-roofed in 1396 using six oak trees to make shingles, and 7,800 nails at 3d. a hundred.

11 A typical Cowper escutcheon on estate cottages at Tewin.

Workmen's Homes

From the early 19th century, with the advent of cheap bricks and improved transport for materials, we have durable housing for agricultural labourers. The cottages in Mill Lane, Welwyn, used, surprisingly, London stock bricks and Welsh slate roofs in 1821. Many of the cottages built on the estates of the Cowpers and their relatives are notable for their yellow brick (allegedly imported from abroad) and their dated 'escutcheon' plaques.

Three

Settlements

Early Prehistory

The evidence for early human activity in the area consists mostly of the scattered finds of nomadic hunter-gatherers, flint tools of the Old Stone Age in the river gravels, and mesolithic flints. Polished flint axes are what remains of the first settlers, farmers of the neolithic period about 6,000 years ago, who lived on the chalk, which provides a well-drained alkaline subsoil that formed light soils which retain their fertility. The Bronze Age is represented by a cremation burial of Beaker date found at Dawley Wood, 'Deverel-Rimbury' pottery in Digswell Water gravel pit, a spear head at Sewells Orchard (Tewin), a broken 'celt' in Sherrardspark Wood, and a number of barb-and-

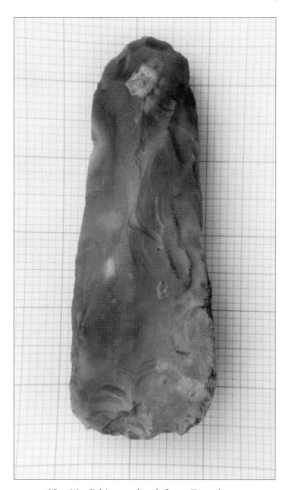

12   Neolithic axe-head from Danesbury.

13   Bronze-Age arrowhead from Digswell.

12

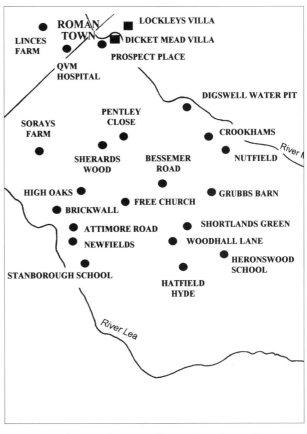

14 The 'Panshanger' Belgic chieftain's burial, now on display at the British Museum. In the background are amphorae, or imported Roman wine jars. The silver cup in the foreground is Neapolitan.

15 Map showing the sites of known Iron-Age and Belgic (dots) and Roman (squares) settlements in the area.

tanged arrowheads. A hoard of bronze implements was found in Welwyn.

The Belgae

Local gravels are mainly a mixture of flint stones with sand, like concrete 'aggregate' or 'road hoggin', for which purposes they were used. They are not acid, and with good husbandry yield reasonably fertile soils, but because they were more difficult to clear of wildwood than the chalk soils, and needed coulter ploughs for cultivation, they were not exploited until the arrival at the beginning of the first century B.C. of the Belgae, Iron-Age people from the continent. Discoveries during the construction of the new town indicate that the land on the plateau between the Lea and the Mimram was

cleared of forest and cultivated from many small farms, each enclosed by a ditch, thereby inaugurating two thousand years of arable history.

The rich cremation burial of an important person, usually referred to as a 'chieftain', was discovered in 1966 by the author in Daniells. The burial, with imported Roman amphorae (wine jars), a silver cup and other rich grave goods is now on display in the British Museum, along with objects from similar burials found during road diversion at Prospect Place, Welwyn, sixty years earlier, including iron firedogs and stand, two silver cups, and amphorae.

The Romans

Only one of the Iron-Age farmsteads, at Lockleys, is known to have developed into a Roman villa,

16   The third-century Roman baths at Welwyn during excavation in 1970.

although finds indicate that scattered occupation and cultivation continued all over the area into the Roman period. Roman pottery and tiles were found at Crookhams; Stanborough School and Pentley Close sites yielded cremation burials of this period, and at Brickwall Hill a ditch was found which contained a large quantity of first-century Roman pottery. But so far no substantial Roman building has been found in the Garden City. Was there a central villa on the plateau from which the whole area was administered?

At Welwyn there was a small Roman town, a posting station on the main road from Verulamium to Puckeridge. Foundations of substantial buildings have been found in the grounds of the Manor House, and straggling occupation along the road as far as Broomfield Road. There were three cemeteries, the largest of which, at The Grange, contained some four thousand burials. In addition to Lockleys a large villa has been partially excavated at Dicket Mead. One suite of its baths was preserved by the author and is displayed today under the A1(M).

Saxons

After the Roman administration failed, it is unlikely that land already cultivated by Britons and Romans became deserted. Settlement reverted instead to small, self-sufficient communities, hamlets around mainly triangular greens. Some of these grew, but some have disappeared and appear as 'greens' and 'ends' on modern maps. Tewin had at least four greens. Like most of the county, our area was rural. It grew and processed crops for itself. Modern hamlets grew around the mills and fords, as at Lemsford Mills or Mill Green.

We can often deduce from other sources where settlements existed but, because the Saxons used materials which were mainly 'bio-degradable', there is a dearth of archaeological evidence for the 'sub-Roman' or Early Saxon periods. Christian burials of seventh-century date have been discovered at Welwyn, however, and there was a monasterium there (a 'group-practice' of priests) in the tenth century.

Early Roads

For most of the history of human settlement tracks were used by people on foot and their animals. We can only speculate on the routes of most minor prehistoric trackways, but it seems clear that in our area long-distance routes went along the river valleys. These were the prototypes, for example, of the Kimpton Road at Welwyn and the B1000 along the Mimram, and the A414 along the Lea. In Iron-Age times a cross-country route connected important settlements at Prae Wood (St Albans), Wheathampstead, Welch's Farm (Burnham Green) and Braughing. It forded the Mimram where Welwyn is now.

The Roman government of Britain relied upon a network of good roads which were suitable for wheeled vehicles, especially between administrative centres. The main routes through Hertfordshire were radial from London. Our area lies between Watling Street to the west and Ermine Street to the east. It is significant that there was no equivalent of the later Great North Road, and there is no evidence for any Roman settlement at Hatfield, south of which was thickly forested.

The site of Welwyn village was a suitable place to ford the River Mimram, at the crossing of two steep-sided valleys, each of which provided a natural route of communication. The only undisputed main road in our area was probably created, therefore, by straightening and draining the ancient route between what had become Verulamium and the town at Wickham Hill (Puckeridge). This improved road ran in a series of straight lines, passing down beside School Lane, where a settlement grew, under Welwyn church and along the modern B196 to Robbery Bottom, before turning onto the second alignment alongside Datchworth Green to Watton at Stone. Air photography and recent excavations have shown that the side ditches of this road were a surprising 90 feet (27m.) apart, but suggest that much of this width was not substantially metalled. The prehistoric river routes continued in use.

The alignments of a number of Roman roads have been postulated in our area, but there is little or no archaeological evidence for them, or their purpose. It is likely that, with dredging and maintenance, the Mimram and the Lea were capable of transporting heavy loads, particularly cereals.

After the end of Roman administration in the fifth century, settlements became self-sufficient and journeys of any length uncommon. With neglect and the advent of watermills, the rivers ceased to be navigable. For a thousand years there was no effective maintenance of roads. They wore their way into the landscape to become muddy 'sunken ways' on which wheeled vehicles were almost useless. Main roads had little or no function, although chance meant some stretches remained in use. The Roman road between Water End and School Lane vanished, the Saxons preferring routes near to the bottom of the valley. The section from the top of Church Street to Robbery Bottom stayed in use but was rerouted into the valley.

The existence of the village in the Dark Ages is problematical. Although there was a monasterium here, no market developed, and the medieval road pattern, which can be deduced from early maps and from fieldwork, suggests that travellers found it

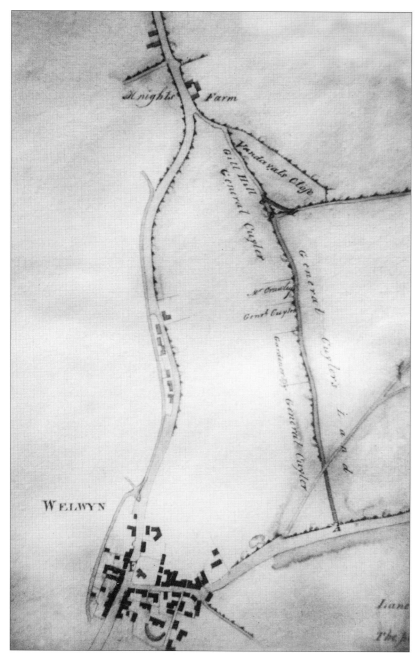

17 Map showing Gill Hill, an alternative and probably older route taken by the Codicote (or Bedford) road north of Welwyn village.

more convenient to avoid the ford (and hence the present High Street) than to go through it. London Road was a dauntingly steep hill, leading to the mire (Mountain Slough) further south. The Hertford Road came through Lockleys and joined the Codicote Road, which came over Danesbury (Gill Hill) at the east end of Church Street. The Kimpton Road continued south-eastwards (behind the cemetery) to join what is now School Lane at Ellesfield.

Hatfield, which lies some distance from the prehistoric track along the Lea Valley and, with no obvious north-south road, would seem to have been

In *WELGE* ten qdā pbr . I . hid in elemofina de rege . Tra . ē
. III . car . In dnio . ē una . 7 alia pot fieri . Ibi . vi . bord hnt
. I . car . Ibi . II . cot . Ptū . I . car . Paftura ad pecun . Silua . L . porc.
Int totū ual 7 ualuit fep . xxv . fol . Iftemet tenuit de rege . E.

18 Domesday Survey entry for Welwyn: 'In Welwyn a priest holds one hide, in alms from the king ...'. The rector is still lord of the manor.

even more of a dead end at this time. However, it was given some importance by becoming a holding of the powerful monastery of Ely whose tenants were required, in the 13th century, to transport goods to and from London and Kelshall.

Normans

The English surrendered to the Normans in 1066 at Little Berkhamsted. The despoliation as the invading army swept round London may have been responsible for a drop of about a half in local land values which followed. Welwyn was reduced by 43 per cent, Hatfield by 17 per cent and Tewin by 50 per cent.

This information was recorded in 1086, 20 years after the Conquest, when the Normans compiled the first overall survey of the country in Domesday Book, which provided details of each 'vill'. A vill was not a village. Nor was a manor a single coherent area of land with a 'manor house' as its centre; it was the place at which taxation was collected. Hatfield is referred to as a manor and there is a manor at Tewin, but land was often 'held' by manors which was located in distant vills. For example, Welwyn had one holding 'in' Weston and another 'in' Bygrave, while part of Chells (Stevenage) is 'in' Welwyn and part of Tewin in 'a ranch (hardwich) of Stevenage'.

What the Domesday Commissioners were interested in were assets and their potential input to the exchequer. Although the survey did not produce a map, it gives us an idea of the relative areas of the vills, which it measures in 'hides'. The hide is often taken to be 120 acres but was not a statutory area; rather, it represented enough land to support a household. The amount of arable and woodland can be deduced from the number of ploughs, and the number of pigs which were fed on the pannage.

Four

Churches, Fields, Farms and Inns

Religion

We have tantalising evidence of religious, magical or superstitious beliefs in the furnishing of the Iron-Age chieftain's burial at Grubs Barn, in the grave

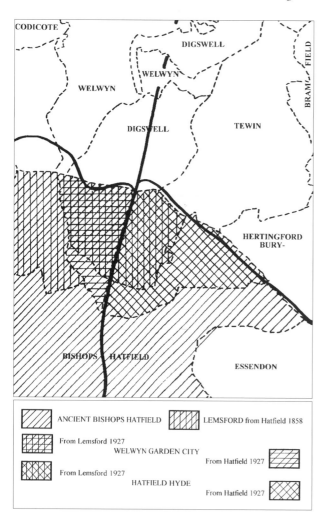

19 Map showing the creation of new parishes.

goods (and a possible mausoleum-temple) in the Roman cemeteries, and in a Graeco-Egyptian amulet from the Roman villa at Dicket Mead. The place-name Tewin is believed to derive from that of a pagan Saxon god. There is, however, no evidence of communal worship before the Christian Saxon period.

Skeletons believed to be of Christians were excavated at The Grange, Welwyn, and dated to A.D.675, suggesting a possible continuity of Christian worship on the site from the Roman period. Aethelgifu, a Saxon noblewoman, left a bequest to the monasterium there in about 985. A 'priest' was lord of the manor in 1086.

The original ecclesiastical parishes in our area of study were Welwyn, Tewin, Digswell and Hatfield. Later parishes were created out of the northern part of Hatfield at Lemsford, and then at Welwyn Garden City and Hatfield Hyde.

Tiles salvaged from the Roman town were used in the construction of an early church on the site of St Mary the Virgin at Welwyn, just as they were at St Alban's Abbey, and Norman work is also reported to have been discovered during restoration. The church's foundation is attributed to Gunnora de Valognes in the late 12th century, but there is little to be seen of early work. The chancel arch is 13th-century, and the piscina is possibly slightly later; the displaced rood screen and carved Totternhoe corbels are 15th-century. A Frythe chapel was added at the south-east corner in 1868, and the church was extended at the west end in 1911, when a new tower was built and all the external walls, except those of the Frythe chapel, were replaced. There has been a great deal of heavy-handed, if tasteful, restoration.

18

20 One of the Saxon burials found beneath The Grange, Welwyn and radiocarbon dated to *c*.A.D.675. Their orientation and lack of grave goods identifies the burials as Christian.

21 Watercolour by J.C. Buckler of Welwyn church in 1832. Although parts of this structure survive inside, the exterior has been entirely rebuilt on a larger scale.

22   The rear of Welwyn church before the extensive restoration in 1911.

St Etheldreda's (or Audry's) of Hatfield is dedicated to the founder of the religious house at Ely, and it is surprising, since the manor was given to the monastery by Edgar, that nothing Saxon or Norman is visible in the structure. The earliest monument, not *in situ*, is that of an armed warrior, dated to about 1190. Like St Mary's at Welwyn, the church has been much restored. The nave was rebuilt, the windows changed from Perpendicular to Decorated, and the chancel arch narrowed in 1872. The interior contains a great deal of genuine antiquity and interest from the 13th century onwards, including the Salisbury chapel and the astonishing monument to the first earl it was built to house. The tower is medieval, and once had a spire which was taken down in the 18th century. A second spire, erected in 1847, was taken down again in 1930.

St Peter's at Tewin is supposed to have been founded by Peter de Valognes in about 1086, and it contains 11th-century work. The chancel was remodelled in the 13th century when the south aisle was added. The tower is probably of the 15th century.

23   The church at Ayot St Peter after it was struck by lightning in 1874.

Until recently it was believed that St John's at Digswell was built in the 12th century, its establishment being attributed to Geoffrey de Mandeville, who granted it to the monasterium at Walden. However, the discovery by the author of an 11th-century arch apparently inserted into the north wall of the nave suggests a much earlier foundation. The piscina is 13th-century, and the screen from about 1450. There have been many alterations and restorations.

Land Lords

Thanks to Domesday Book, we can deduce who held what land in 1086 with varying degrees of confidence. Hertingfordbury, a five-hide vill on the east side of the site of the future Garden City, was held by Ralph Baynard. There was land for 10 ploughs and forest for 200 pigs. Hatfield, part of which formed most of the southern portion of our area, was held by the Abbots of Ely and was a very large holding: 40 hides. Much of it was forest, enough for 2,000 pigs to roam, but there was a large area of arable, enough for 30 ploughs.

Ayot St Peter, a much smaller vill at two-and-a-half hides, was held, possibly illegally, by Robert Gernon, whose tenant was William. There was land for four ploughs and woodland for 150 pigs. Digswell, with an area of three hides, with land for five ploughs and woodland for 150 pigs, was held partly by Thorkell (probably a Saxon) from Geoffrey de Mandeville, and partly by Roger from Peter de Valognes, who probably also held – with some dispute – the contiguous south side of Tewin, five-and-a-half hides with land for five-and-a-half ploughs.

In Welwyn, which had a total area of seven-and-a-half hides, much of it arable, with 17 ploughs but woodland for only 70 pigs, there were six estates,

24 Aerial view of Hatfield House, the Old Palace, the Gate House and the church from the west.

25 A 19th-century watercolour by J.C. Buckler showing Hatfield Market House after it was moved to the top of Fore Street.

26 The Old Cottage, Bridge Road before the Garden City developed around it.

but within our area of study it is only possible to locate approximately two of them. At least part of the populous two-hide holding of Geoffrey de Bec probably included some of the present village, as he owned the mill. It seems likely that his lands included the area which became the sub-manor of Lockleys, the largest part of Welwyn in our area of study. The Rectory manor, of one hide, with few residents, was held by 'a priest'. His land, which included woodland for 50 pigs, may have been scattered. In later years the rich living was to attract clergy of high standing.

Hatfield grew outside the gates of a powerful landlord. It was granted a royal charter in 1278 permitting weekly markets and an annual fair. A typical medieval market house is shown at the bottom of Fore Street on an old map; it had to be removed to the top when the Great North Road was widened and rerouted. Markets brought prosperity. The Cecils leased the market to tenants – in 1648 for £13 per year for 60 years, for example. It continued until the mid-19th century, when it moved to the cattle and corn market beside the railway opposite the *Red Lion*.

Most of the mainly scattered buildings which existed within the area of the Garden City at the beginning of the 20th century have been destroyed and no proper record survives. Digswell House and some of its associated houses and lodges in Digswell Park Road are still there, as is Digswell Place, once the rectory and still containing 16th-century features. The Old Cottage in Bridge Road is a brick structure dated to 1604, and on the other side of the road is a pair of Cowper cottages in typical yellow brick-work with the crest.

The Vineyard Barn, a community hall also used as a church, is part of Digswell Lodge Farm, which appears on a 1599 map. Lower Handside Farm-house, later converted to a hostel by the New Towns Trust, is now apartments in Barn Court; the Barn Theatre was its dairy. The Backhouse Rooms were a cart shed at Upper Handside Farm. Brickwall Farm House, a home for the elderly, was demolished in 2000. Attimore Hall Farmhouse is now a public house. Some of its barns survive and are used by the Arts Trust, and the *Beehive* was once both pub and general store. Nearby is Ludwick Hall, centre of a sub-manor.

27 Digswell Lodge Farm. Only the barn survives, as a public hall called Vineyard Barn. The new town development can be seen in the background.

28 Attimore Farm. The farmhouse is now a public house.

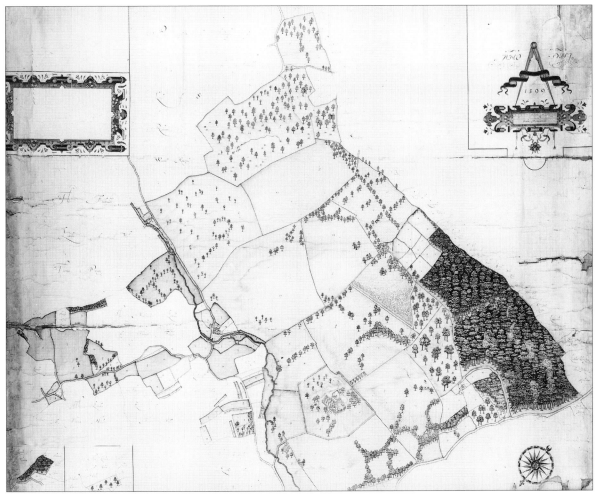

29 The magnificent 1599 map of Digswell. North is towards the bottom left-hand corner, where the Great North Road can be seen.

Fields, Hydes and Farms

It is not until 1599 that we have our earliest accurate cartography in the magnificent survey made then of Digswell estate. Thereafter some detail is provided by manuscript maps but the Tithe Apportionment Act of 1837 required every parish to be accurately surveyed. By patching together the maps produced as a result we can obtain the first detailed field map of our entire area of study. This is an eloquent document.

At a glance one can see that there are areas where field sizes and field shapes differ. For example, there are many small fields packed together in the north of Hatfield parish while, over the border

in Digswell and Tewin, the fields are larger, more rectangular. Each Saxon vill had comprised several large, common fields, within which each peasant cultivated several narrow strips of varying size called 'acres'. The usual explanation for their creation is that each represented one day's ploughing. Their length was as far as the plough-team could go without a rest (a furrow-long, or furlong). So the size depended upon two factors: the heaviness of the soil and the way the fields fitted together.

Hatfield had been given to the monks of Ely in the tenth century as a source of timber and Domesday Book confirms that it was wooded. The geological map shows that much of the land was

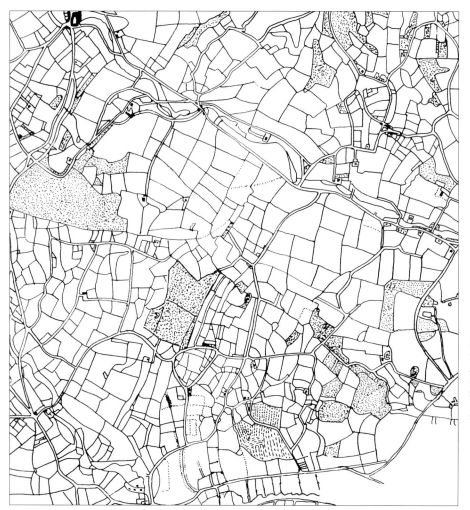

30 Field boundaries as marked on the Tithe Apportionment maps of around 1840. Note the small fields in what was Hatfield parish in the south.

heavy boulder clay. But during the Middle Ages the population increased and more land on the north side of the Lea had to be cultivated. Some became common fields; some was brought into cultivation from the woodland by independent yeomen farmers who made clearings, or 'assarts', with the permission of the lord of the manor, the Prior. The soil was heavy, making for short furrows, and as there was no compulsion to share, it was not farmed in strips. The assarts therefore consisted of small, often irregular, fields. Each assart supported one household and so was called a 'hide' (or 'hyde'), often named after the man who made the clearing. In our area were Ludwick Hyde, Holwell Hyde, Handside, Durants Hyde (now

Brocket Park), Dogen Hyde and Hatfield Hyde (also known as West Hyde). The locations of some hides, whose names are documented, are unknown. Perhaps Woodhall was one of the hides, The Frythe another.

Strip cultivation slowly disappeared as a result of land exchange, inheritance and purchase, and the strips came together into larger holdings. The landlords constructed farmhouses and farmyards but frequently changed the boundaries of the land which went with them. By the time of the conception of Welwyn Garden City, almost the whole of the area was owned by two estates: that of Lord Desborough, and that of Lord Salisbury. The farmers were tenants, who largely resented the purchase over their

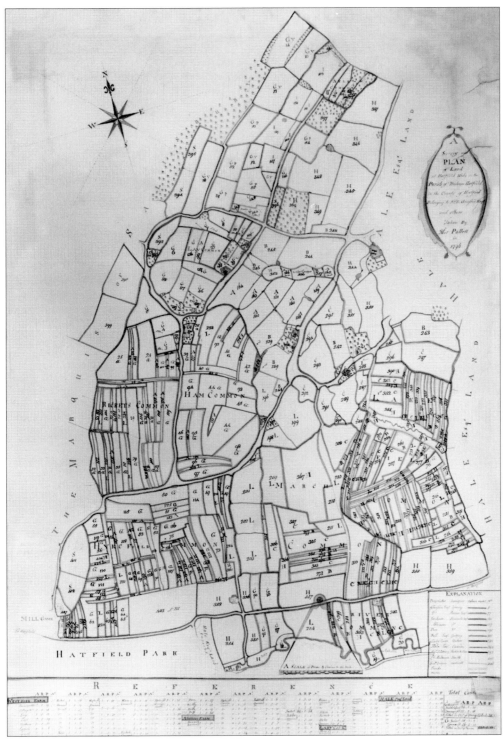

31 A map of 1796 showing strip fields in the area which is now Hatfield Hyde, the Commons and Hall Grove. The Queen Elizabeth II Hospital is in the field marked L.199 near the centre.

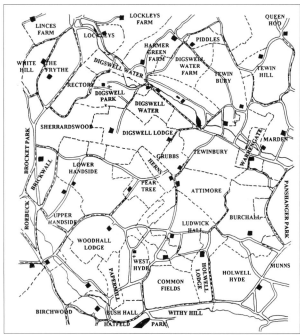

33 Map showing the various farms in the area at the start of the 20th century.

32 Houses at Hatfield Hyde in the early 20th century.

heads of the land for purposes other than farming. James Hunter of Peartree insisted on occupation of his farmhouse and on having an insulation area round it. Most of the other farmers moved away as soon as they could.

Exceptional were the Horn family of Upper and Lower Handside Farms, who gave invaluable agricultural advice to the Garden City Company. W.J. Horn was a County alderman; his son W.C. Horn became a civic director of the Company, a member of the civil Parish Council when it was constituted in 1921, and the first chairman of the Urban District Council in 1927.

Towns

Welwyn only began to become a substantial settlement in the 17th century. Few significant town houses were built there, and expansion was severely restricted by two factors: the steepness of the surrounding hills, and the parks at the Manor House,

34 An early 19th-century picture of Stanborough Farmhouse.

35 Welwyn village from the south in 1967. Since this photograph was taken there has been development on Danesbury, west of the High Street, and at the end of Mimram Road.

36 An aerial photograph of Welwyn village in 1926. This tiny settlement was the centre of rural, postal and police districts. The new by-pass is in the foreground.

37 Welwyn High Street from the north, decorated for the coronation of King Edward VII in 1902. What is most notable is how little this scene has changed.

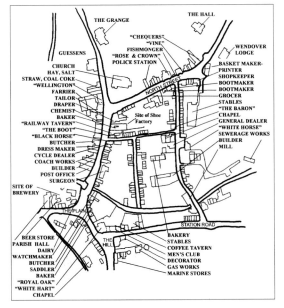

38 Commercial premises in Welwyn village in the early 20th century.

Danesbury, Lockleys and The Frythe. Lockleys built cottages on the east side of Mill Lane for its workers in the 1820s, and development received a much-needed boost in the 1830s between the High Street and Mill Lane after the new rectory was built on glebe land west of the river and infilling took place in the grounds of the old Rectory.

The settlement never broke out of the confines of the Mimram valley until council estates were constructed along London Road and School Lane at Broomfield in the 1930s, at Hawbush, begun in 1950, and Queensway, begun in 1954. The 200th post-war house built by Welwyn Rural District Council was completed in Wilshere Road in November 1953. One social consequence of housing policy was that indigenous people moved out of the meaner dwellings in the centre, which eventually became much sought-after by outsiders. The private development on Danesbury began in 1967.

An unplanned and unregulated sprawling development scattered in the woods to the north-east of the village began between the wars. The opening of the by-pass, however, preserved the physical structure of the core of the village. But the motor car, which brought the new settlers, coupled with the growth of the new town was to lead to Welwyn's

To BUILDERS, CAPITALISTS, and Others

HATFIELD, HERTS.

VOTES FOR THE COUNTY,

ELIGIBLE

FREEHOLD PROPERTY,

PRODUCING RENTALS AMOUNTING TO
£150 PER ANNUM,

COMPRISING A MODERN BRICK-BUILT AND SLATED

VILLA RESIDENCE

With walled Garden, Chaise-house, and Stable,
EIGHT MESSUAGES OR TENEMENTS
AND ABOUT SEVEN ACRES OF

FREEHOLD BUILDING GROUND,

Pleasantly situate within five minutes' walk of the Town of Hatfield, and near the proposed Railway Station commanding a view of the town, the surrounding country, and Hatfield Park, adjoining the high road leading from Hatfield to St Alban's: also,

TWO COTTAGES, IN PARK STREET;
WHICH WILL BE SOLD BY AUCTION, BY
Mr. JACKSON,

AT THE RED LION INN, HATFIELD,

On WEDNESDAY, April 19, 1848, at Two o'clock

MR. JACKSON most respectfully and urgently invites the attention of Speculatists, Builders, Capitalists and others, to the unusually favourable advantages connected with this truly desirable Property, arising from the very great improvements contemplated as likely to arise in the Town of Hatfield from the London and York Railroad passing through the town; from the demand that exists for Genteel Residences and Cottages; from the difficulty of sites for Building purposes; and from the circumstances that the whole of the property in and near the town is in but very few hands.

39 Advertisement for the land sale at Hatfield Newtown in 1848. The phrase 'Votes for the County' is significant since freehold property entitled the owner to vote. At the time the Chartists were building Heronsgate near Chorleywood for this very reason.

decline as an economic or administrative centre. The main post office and police station moved to Welwyn Garden City in 1933 and the Rural District Council ceased to exist in 1974. Many shops, unable to pay the high rates or compete with the easily accessible 'retail outlets' in and outside the towns, have closed, along with many small industries and crafts. The end of the 20th century saw the infilling of gardens and back yards with expensive housing.

40 The original Salisbury Square, built for the staff of the militia between 1850-3. The steps, called 'Jacob's Ladder', provided a short cut to the church.

41 A late 19th-century view of Arm and Sword Yard, Hatfield. This ran between North Road and Park Street, opposite the station.

Expansion of Hatfield town was restricted only to the east by the presence of Hatfield House and Park, and the town was, somewhat surprisingly, not owned by the Cecils. Much of it was freehold, as was the land to the west, and could be used for building. In 1847, just before the railway arrived, a piece of land between St Albans Road and Wellfield Road was advertised for building. The opening words of the advertisement, 'Votes for the County', were particularly significant at this time; Heronsgate near Chorleywood, for example, was being developed by the Chartists with enfranchisement as the main object. Newtown, also known as 'California' because it was a wild west place, soon attracted its own shops and pubs. Many of its early inhabitants were displaced from the area when the original Salisbury Square was created to house the staff of the militia in 1850-3. This site, now part of

42 Commercial premises in Hatfield in the early 20th century.

43 Wrestlers' Bridge, Hatfield, after the collapse in February 1966 which cut off the old Great North Road. It was replaced by a pedestrian bridge.

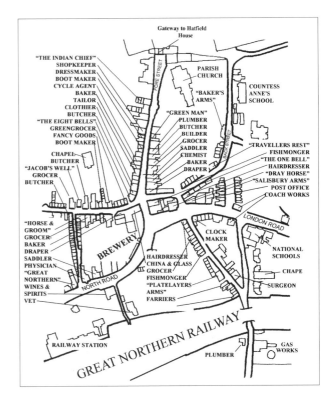

44 Early 20th-century postcard view of Hatfield. The Great North Road is to the right and Fore Street to the left. The brewery was behind the wall on the left.

Hatfield New Town, is, ironically, referred to as 'Hatfield Town Centre'.

Hatfield developed westwards. The police headquarters and courthouse were built on St Albans Road. Barnet by-pass opened in 1928 and took away the Great North Road traffic, and the aircraft works and associated development followed. In 1949 Hatfield New Town (which is outside the scope of this book) was begun. In 1966 Wrestlers' Bridge, which had carried the road to the north of the town, collapsed. Demolition and alteration by the developers made the old town unrecognisable.

Routes

When maps were first made, roads were rarely marked. Long-distance travel was rare; most journeys were limited to going to and from work in the fields, or to market. A decree by Elizabeth I that made the vestries responsible for highways had little effect, especially in parishes with small labour forces and little stone. But by this time the wear and tear on roads in Hertfordshire was exacerbated by the movement of farm produce, especially from the north-east of the county and from Cambridgeshire and Bedfordshire, and by the large numbers of animals 'on the hoof' – from great distances, even Scotland – to market in London.

The Great North Road

By the end of the 17th century changing attitudes and the introduction of the coach encouraged the gentry to make longer journeys. The 'North Road' up the Lea valley through Ware was choked and muddied by commercial traffic. Hatfield Palace now required a good road to London, which, with the arrival of the coaching

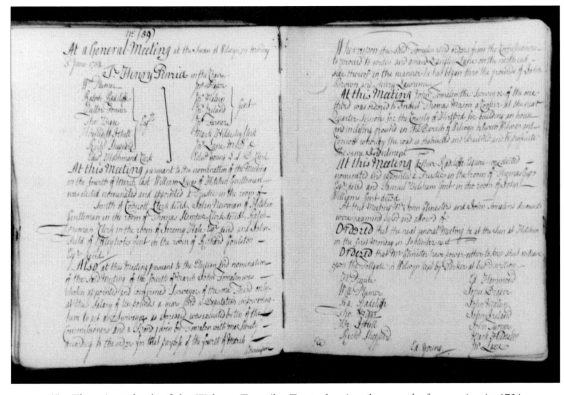

45   The minute book of the Welwyn Turnpike Trust, showing the record of a meeting in 1734.

era, joined an improvised route to Welwyn and thereby became the Great North Road. Until the mid-19th century, then, the main road led to Hatfield House, from which it went into the town down the very steep Fore Street, which required skid pans to descend and often auxiliary horses to ascend. After two sharp turns it went down Lizard Lane (where, later, the brewery was). From there it followed the ancient Lea valley route to Lemsford, and then took a very difficult way: up beside the wall of Brocket Park (hence 'Brickwall Hill') to Ayot Green and down a steep muddy valley ('Mountain Slough') into Welwyn village. This route radically affected our area. The prosperity of Hatfield and Welwyn became linked by the road and both became major coaching centres, providing refreshments and changes of horses. In 1663 an appeal for the rebuilding of Welwyn church tower stated that 'persons of great quality come to the church because it is on the Great Road to London'.

At the beginning of the 18th century parliament started appointing 'turnpike trusts', consisting of gentry, clergy and businessmen, which were empowered to collect tolls for the maintenance of specific roads, but it was not until 1726 that the road through Welwyn became 'turnpiked'. There were 'turnpikes' (toll gates) at Hatfield, Ayot Green, Welwyn and Woolmer Green.

Hostelries

Posting stations needed inns. At Welwyn *The Swan* and *The Boar's Head* were in existence in the 16th century. Later, they amalgamated and became *The Wellington*. A private dwelling became the *White Hart* in about 1675; it was extended in 1756 to provide a courthouse and a banqueting room which was later used as Village Institute and the District Council chamber. The *Red Lion* (on the site of the chemist's shop) is mentioned in 1688, and the *Rose and Crown* in 1633. By the 19th century there were at least twenty licensed premises in the parish of

46 The old turnpike-keeper's cottage opposite Ayot Green shortly before it was demolished to make way for the A1(M) motorway in 1969.

47 The *Salisbury Temperance Hotel*, Great North Road, Hatfield in the early 20th century.

Welwyn, mainly in the village or along the main roads through it, and the motoring age between the wars produced new 'road houses'. At Stanborough a new *Bull* was built on the opposite side of the North Road from its predecessor. The *North Star* at Mardley Hill and *The Clock* date from this time, and there were several more cafés, teashops and restaurants which have since disappeared.

In Hatfield, too, the rise of the road caused the number of public houses to increase; 23 are listed in the 19th century. Several became hotels. The *Gate House* at the top of Fore Street became the *Salisbury Arms* in about 1725, and had stabling for 100 horses; it is mentioned by Pepys, Smollett, Dickens and Jane Austen.

When the railway was mooted, the Rev. F.J. Faithful, rector of the parish church, argued that the railway would provide cheap coal and 'the scarcity of coal has an unfavourable effect on the inhabitants' morals. It drives them from their houses to seek comfort in public houses and places of questionable resort.' The railway opened in 1850, and the following year eight new public houses opened in the town! A new *Salisbury Temperance Hotel* was also built on the new London Road.

There was an alehouse in Digswell in 1806, but its location is unknown. A public house at Cobble End probably became the *Railway Tavern* in 1851 and was renamed the *Cowper Arms Hotel* in 1871. It is, perhaps, surprising that there are no pubs recorded along the road from Welwyn to Hertford, but it is not obvious what factors influenced the siting of pubs deep in rural areas.

Five

Country Seats

At the beginning of the 20th century there were ten parks or large gardens where the Garden City is today. No fewer than five of them belonged to Earl Cowper: on the east was Panshanger, the family seat; in the middle was Digswell Park; Brocket Park was in the west; and Tewin Water and Marden were in the north.

Panshanger

At one time 'Panshangra' belonged to St Bartholomew's, Smithfield and, until the beginning of the 19th century, was mostly common agricultural land. It was bought in 1720 by William Cowper, Lord Chancellor, who had been created Viscount Fordwich and Earl Cowper by George I two years earlier. He built a mansion called Cole Green House. His son, the second earl, a Lord of the Bedchamber as well as Lord-Lieutenant and Custos Rotulorum for Hertfordshire, was succeeded in turn by his son, George Nassau Clavering. He had been M.P. for Hertford from 1759 to 1761 but, upon inheriting, spent most of the rest of his

48 19th-century painting of Panshanger House.

life in Italy. He was a famous connoisseur and collector of paintings. His eldest son, the fourth earl, George Augustus, died unmarried and was succeeded by his brother, Peter Leopold Lewis Francis.

The fifth earl set about purchasing land, and by the time of his death held most of the valley of the river Mimram from Hertford to Welwyn and three-quarters of the land on which Welwyn Garden City was eventually to be built. He demolished Cole Green House and, by diverting roads and footpaths, created Panshanger Park and built Panshanger House – a castellated gothic pile designed by William Atkins – in 1806-20. Queen Victoria visited it in 1841. The park was land-scaped by Humphry Repton and his 'Red Book', outlining the design, including that of the house, still survives.

Peter Leopold married Emily Lamb, daughter of Peniston Lamb, 1st Viscount Melbourne, in 1805 and eventually became brother-in-law to Queen Victoria's favourite Prime Minister, who lived at Brocket Park. Two years after his death in 1839 Emily married Lord Palmerston and so, having been the sister of one Prime Minister, she became wife of another.

The earldom and subsidiary titles became extinct with the death of the seventh earl in 1905. The last Countess Cowper lived at Panshanger until she died in 1913, when the estate was inherited by Lord Desborough through the countess' niece, Lady Desborough. The family lost two sons during the First World War, and in 1919 death duties compelled the sale of the outlying portions of the estate at which Ebenezer Howard made his purchase. After the death of Lady Desborough in 1952 the house was demolished and the park was bought by a gravel company.

Digswell

Digswell became one estate in 1227 when William de Mandeville, Earl of Essex, married Christiana de Valognes, who also owned Lockleys. It is likely that a later tenant of Digswell was largely responsible for setting the scene for the development of the north-western part of Welwyn Garden City – by removing the villagers in order to create a park. He is Lawrence de St Michael, who inherited in 1283.

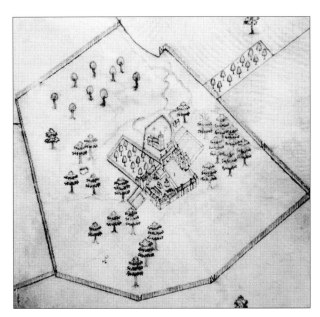

49 Detail of the 1599 Digswell map showing, within the park pale, the church and house demolished by Earl Cowper in 1803.

When the settlement first began, the manor house and the church were the centre of the village. In 1285 we read of Lawrence stopping up a path through Sherrardspark Wood and creating another; in 1291 he closed the path through Church Grove. There is no mention of houses or people, but we may assume that the nucleus of the settlement moved to Digswell Water, close to the mill. When the land was bought by Howard in 1919, Digswell Park Road still made a great loop to distance itself from Digswell House and the church beside it. This feature, with an earlier Digswell House, can be seen on the map of 1599, along with concentric high fences – a park pale.

Digswell was owned in the 15th and 16th centuries, along with Lockleys, Ayot St Peter, Ludwick, Holwell and parts of Tewin and Welwyn, by the Perient family. It belonged to the Shallcross family from 1656 until 1785, when it was bought by the 3rd Earl Cowper. The medieval house was demolished in 1803 by the fifth earl, who built the present classical one and set about diverting rights of way and creating an ornamental lake. The lake was cut off from the house when Bessemer Road was extended to the

50 Old cottages at Digswell Water. These are now one house with a large central gable and a huge extension.

51 Digswell House in use as an army hospital in the First World War.

Hertford Road, and the lake and surrounding land was leased to the Digswell Lake Society which maintains it as a park for enjoyment. The Society now owns the park. At the time of Howard's purchase, the tenant was Col. Acland, who greatly resented Desborough's sale.

Lockleys

Lockleys was a sub-manor held in 1303 for a quarter knight's fee from Agnes de Valognes. In 1399 it passed from John of Gaunt to Henry IV. The present house was built for Edward Searle in 1717. He diverted the Hertford Road away from the house and built 'pleasure gardens'. George Shee bought the property in 1812 and diverted the road again to enlarge the park. One of his descendents was George Dering, an inventor and Fellow of the Royal Society, whose diversion of the road led to the digging of a deep cutting out of Welwyn. In his later years he neglected the estate, and it was discovered at his death that he was married and had a wife and daughter in Brighton, where he was known as Mr. Dale. His daughter, Mrs. Rosa Neale, who leased the house to Sir Evelyn de la Rue, transferred the estate to her son Richard, who sold it to the

52 Lady de la Rue on the 'bowling alley' at Lockleys in 1917.

53 Brocket Hall in a painting by John Charnock of 1780.

54 Joseph Sabine and his family in front of Tewin Mansion.

Welwyn Garden City Company in 1936. It was leased to St Margaret's Girl's School, who let it to ICI as a hostel during the Second World War. In 1955 it was bought as a boarding house and junior school by Sherrardswood School. The senior school moved from the Garden City to a new building in the grounds in 1995.

Brocket Hall

Brocket Park was created by the Brocket family largely from the holding called Durants Hyde. The present house was constructed for Sir Matthew Lamb by Thomas Paine in about 1760-75. In 1756 he became a Baronet, and in 1770 Prime Minister. In the same year he took the title Lord Melbourne – an Irish Viscountcy did not prevent him sitting in the House of Commons. His son William Lamb married Caroline Ponsonby. Famous for her infatuation with Lord Byron, she died in 1828.

William became successively Irish Secretary, Foreign Secretary and Prime Minister, and Brocket Hall was visited by Queen Victoria in 1841. He died in 1848 and his sister, Emily, widow of the 5th Earl Cowper, inherited and married Lord Palmerston, by whom she had, it is said, already borne 'more then

one' child. Thus, as we have seen, Brocket was the home of two Prime Ministers. Its various tenants included Admiral Walter Kerr, who was the husband of Annabel, sister of the 7th Earl Cowper, who built several estate cottages in typical 'Cowper' style but with 'WK' on the escutcheons. Brocket was sold by the Cowpers to Charles Nall-Cain in 1922. Today, following the conviction of Lord Brocket for fraud, it has become a conference centre. The landscape, by Joseph Wood, is much changed by modern golf-course mania.

Tewin

Tewin, like Panshanger, had once belonged to St Bartholmew's. Another early emparkment seems to have occurred here, as there are centres of settlement around two greens some distance from the church, which stands alone. It is not easy to unravel the historical geography of the parish of Tewin, but it is likely that Tewin House, built by Thomas Montford in 1632, was on the site of the original manor. Its replacement, built for Joseph Sabine after he bought the estate in 1715, stood alone beside the church before the 5th Earl Cowper demolished it in 1805. It is probable that the emparkment was

55 The original design for Tewin Water House, taken from the Red Book by Repton, who includes himself in the bottom left-hand corner.

made by Sabine, whose monument is in the church porch.

Tewin Water

Tewin Water is first mentioned as a 'capital messuage, repaired and beautified' in 1746. One famous owner of the house was Lady Cathcart. The daughter of a brewer, she married James Fleet, who owned Tewin Manor. He died in 1733 leaving her wealthy. She then married Joseph Sabine, who rebuilt Tewin Manor House. After he died in 1739, she married Lord Cathcart, who died within a year. Her next husband, Hugh McGuire, an Irish officer in the Hungarian service, a notorious duellist, carried her off to his ancestral castle in Ireland, where she was held a prisoner for twenty years. In 1766 McGuire died – killed in a duel say some, of lockjaw say others – and Lady Cathcart returned to England. She recovered her property – a contemporary map shows Tewin Water as belonging to both Cathcart and Steele – and became famous for her appearances at balls, assemblies and routs. She died at the age of 97. Her story was the basis of *Castle Rackrent* by Maria Edgeworth. It is said that inside her wedding ring was engraved 'If I survive, I will have five.'

The present house was created for Cowper by John Groves in about 1798, and Repton, who suggested the design of the house and stables, also landscaped the park. This involved diverting the Hertford Road and several footpaths and creating a lake. After having been a school for the deaf, the house is now central to new residential development.

Marden

Marden was probably the holding of Tova, widow of Wihtric, in about 1050; she paid the Abbot of St Albans at the annual Feast of St Peter ad Vincula one sextar and 32 ounces of honey that she and her son should hold it for the rest of their lives, after which it should pass to St Albans without contradiction. At the Dissolution of the Monasteries

56   An early engraving of Hatfield House.

it passed to William Cavendish. The present house was built in 1790-4 by Francis Carter for Robert Macky, and improved by Sir John Soane in 1819. It was purchased by the 7th Earl Cowper in 1874. Today it is in multiple tenancy.

Hatfield House

Hatfield House was the successor of the Old Palace, built by Cardinal Morton in 1497. In 1514 Henry VIII's farrier was the lessee from the Bishop of Ely, but the King used it virtually as his own. After the Dissolution it became a residence for his children. In 1549 Edward VI granted it to the Earl of Warwick, but Elizabeth managed to retain it by exchanging property. It was here that she was told she had become Queen of England. In 1603 it was 'in dower' for Anne of Denmark.

James I decided to swap it for Theobalds, the residence of Robert Cecil Burghley, the second son of Elizabeth's Chief Minister. As a result Robert, who became Earl of Salisbury and James's Chief Minister, held the manor and three parks, which became joined. He demolished the Palace, leaving only the banqueting hall, which became stables, and built the present house in about 1611. The design was by Robert Lyminge, who was advised by others including, it is said, Inigo Jones. Lord Salisbury died in 1612. The house was visited by James I and by his son Charles while a prisoner on his way to London.

Many of the Salisbury family were notable statesmen. The first marquess was George III's Lord Chamberlain, and the third was Victoria's Prime Minister three times, and was visited by Gladstone, Disraeli and by Lewis Carroll. Under the fourth, Hatfield House was a social and political centre. Balfour, Chamberlain, Kitchener and Edward VII stayed there. Like Digswell House, it was a hospital during the First World War. The fifth was the third successive marquess to be leader of the House of Lords. The family are still in residence.

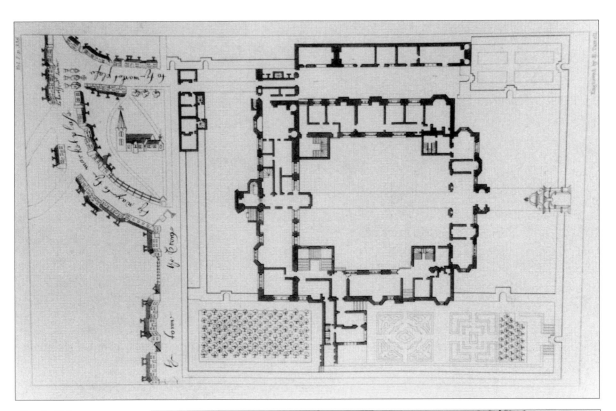

57 A 19th-century engraving of an early plan of Hatfield Palace. Only the west wing, nearest the church, survives. The market house in the town is shown as three separate buildings.

58 An interior view of Woodhall in 1831 by Luppino, a stage set designer. No exterior view has been found.

59   Ludwick Hall before it was surrounded by modern development.

Woodhall

Some of the hides became administrative centres or 'sub-manors'. One that has disappeared but had a considerable effect on the landscape was Hatfield Woodhall. At the time of Edward I it was held by the Bassingburns as a sub-manor of Hatfield, for half a knight's fee, suit of court and tuppence a year. In the reign of Elizabeth I it was in the hands of the Boteler family. In 1690 it passed to a daughter, Julia, widow of Francis Shallcross of Digswell, then to her sister, Isabella Hutchinson. In 1792 the Rev. Julius Hutchinson sold it to the 1st Marquess of Salisbury, who demolished it because, it is alleged, it rivalled Hatfield House in splendour. From the time of the earliest map of the area at the beginning of the 16th century a road has made a great loop round Woodhall. This is represented today by Stanborough Road, Twentieth Mile Bridge, Woodhall Lane and Hollybush Lane. They are the fossil remnants of the emparkment. A similar loop at Hatfield Hyde suggests that there may have been

an emparkment there. Recent development on the site makes archaeological investigation of it virtually impossible.

Ludwick

Ludwick was held in 1176 by Roger de Luda, and later we find William de Luda on a pilgrimage to Santiago with Fitzsimon of Symonshyde. William's son dedicated a chantry altar to St Anne in Hatfield in 1333, but a generation later John and Thomas, his sons, were accused of breaking into Woodhall (and Digswell?), and of poaching royal deer at Cheshunt. The 'manors' of Ludwick Hyde and Holwell Hyde were bought in 1588 from de Lacey for £2,000. In the time of James I Ludwick was held of the Cecils, the lords of the manor-in-chief, for a quarter of a knight's fee, and in 1637 Ludwick is described as 348 acres of land and 50 acres of wood worth £200 per acre. The privately owned house is now surrounded by modern development.

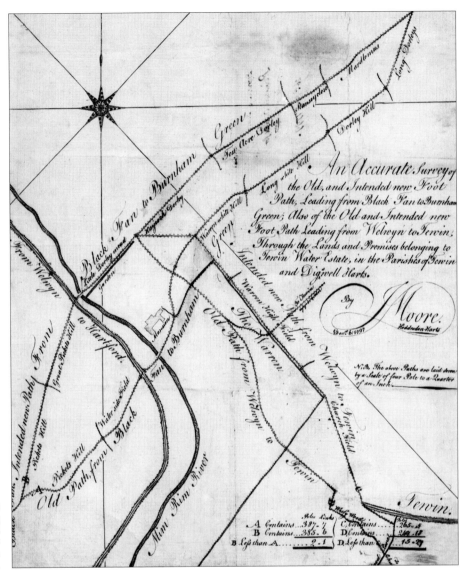

60 Map of Tewin Water in 1797 showing which rights of way Earl Cowper proposed to divert in order to improve the park.

Handside

Handside was held for a quarter knight's fee of the Bishop of Ely in 1324 by John Poleyn, whose wife Anne had a quarter fee in Welwyn, and we can trace its possession to Edward Brocket, who took legal action to possess it. He died seized of it in 1599, when the sub-manor was merged with Brocket. No manor house survives.

The Frythe

The Frythe was probably given to the Priory of Holywell, Shoreditch by Gunnora de Valognes. It was leased by the Wilshere family in the time of Richard II, and had 50 acres of land in 1553. The present house, now surrounded by modern laboratories, was built in 1846. The estate was used for top-secret development work during the Second World War and then leased to ICI, who bought it in 1955. ICI shared it with Unilever for one year from 1963. Unilever were there until 1977, when Smith Klein took over. It is now owned by GlaxoSmithKline.

Welwyn Manor

The original manor house, now the Old Rectory, was built in the late 15th century. Dr. Edward Young, rector from 1730-65, purchased Guessens because the Rectory proved unsuitable for his needs. He had been tutor to Lord Burghley and chaplain to George II and was a playwright and poet (he had refused the post of Poet Laureate in 1729). He influenced the Romantic School of German poets, including Schiller and Goethe. His best-known work is *Night Thoughts on Life, Death and Immortality*, first published in 1750.

At his death his successor, the Rev. Thomas Bathurst, attempted 'reparations' to the original rectory. He died in 1797. In 1772 the Rev. Ralph Freeman, former rector of Ayot St Peter, left in his will £4,000 for amending or building new parsonages at Welwyn and Barking, and what is known today as the Manor House at Welwyn was completed on glebe land in 1798. In the 1880s the Rev. Charles Wingfield rented a house at the top of Hobbs Hills as a summer residence (perhaps to avoid the smell), his sister bought it, and in 1920 it became the Rectory, and the Manor House was sold.

Danesbury

Both name and park at Danesbury are modern inventions. Mary St John built a house there, St John Lodge, in 1775. Her husband, a Royal Navy captain, was killed in action in 1780 and left his property in trust to his son Henry. In 1794 it was put up for sale to pay various legacies, and bought by General Cuyler, who altered the house, diverted roads and created a park and estate of 500 acres. In 1824 it was bought by William Blake, a sitting tenant who remodelled it and renamed it Danesbury. It remained in the Blake family until 1917, when the estate began to be broken up. In 1919 Mrs. Barton sold it to Mr. and Mrs. Michael Dewar, who became notable benefactors of the local church and hospital. They sold the house and gardens to the Middlesex County Council in 1922. Sold to developers in 1994, the house became the centre of a luxury residential development.

Diversions

Emparkment and the improvement of estates were principal causes of diversion of highways and byways as well as removal of villagers. An early 17th-century map of Hatfield in Hatfield House shows the tracks which were to become the 'Lanes' of Welwyn Garden City three hundred years later, but by way of contrast the 1599 map of Digswell shows no roads or even substantial tracks south of the Mimram, apart from the Hertford Road, which is gated, although it clearly indicates a muddy path to the church. By that time the emparkment must have been 300 years old and, as the map shows by means of small symbols, the land was enclosed and in the hands of a few tenants.

The Hertford Road from Welwyn was rerouted three times to move it away from Lockleys house: in about 1720, 1823 and 1906. Earl Cowper also diverted that road – and many lesser tracks, bridlepaths and footpaths – at the beginning of the 19th century as part of the landscaping at Digswell, Tewin Water and Panshanger.

Six

The Public Good

Traditional Industries

Historically, the main industries in our area were milling, malting and brewing. In Domesday Book each vill had its watermill, and multure was the lord's monopoly. On the Mimram there were mills at Codicote, Welwyn, Digswell and Tewin, on the Lea at Lemsford and Mill Green. Flour mills continued to be important until the early years of the 20th century. Water power could be used for purposes other than grinding flour. Fulling mills processed cloth, and in the 18th century Tewin Mill was used to grind spectacle lenses. On the Lea at Hatfield, near Bush Hall, there was a paper-mill from before 1672 until it was destroyed by fire in 1838 and the sawmill at the eastern edge of Hatfield Park was built in 1830.

Malting and brewing were initially cottage industries, but they became progressively centralised.

Malt-making seems to have been for local use, rather than for the London market, as was the case in the rich barley-growing area in the north-east of the county. A brewery was founded in 1833 at the bottom of School Lane, Welwyn by John Cass. Another Welwyn brewer, Benjamin Newton, appears in directories, but the location of his premises is unknown. By 1851 the School Lane brewery was owned by James Deards, who also made barrels. After several lease changes it was bought at the end of the 19th century by McMullens of Hertford, who ceased to brew there, but used it as a store and off-licence until 1947.

Sometime before 1630 Searanck purchased the Chequers and its brewhouse in the centre of Hatfield. From this was to grow one of the largest breweries in the county. In about 1700 John Harrow started another brewery nearby. Eventually the breweries,

61   Digswell Mill before restoration.

49

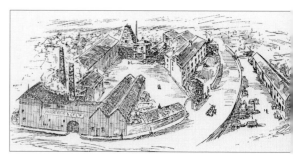

62 Mew's Brewery, at the bottom of School Lane, Welwyn, in around 1920.

63 Hatfield Brewery.

64 Pryor Reid Co.'s steam-driven brewer's dray at the beginning of the 20th century.

65   The *Red Lion*, Digswell Hill at the beginning of the 20th century. The former smithy had become a garage.

separated by Arm and Sword Yard, occupied several acres of the centre of the town in a triangle between Duck Lane (now Park Street) and the North Road. There were also several maltings in the town. The breweries were owned by Pryor in 1840, and then Pryor Reid & Co. and were closed down in 1920. Both Welwyn and Hatfield were well known for their large numbers of public houses.

Until about seventy years ago blacksmiths provided an essential service along the main roads, the pub and the smithy being the equivalent of today's motorway service station. There were smithies at Hatfield, Mill Green, Stanborough, Lemsford, the *Red Lion* (formerly *Leg o' Mutton*) at Ayot Green, Welwyn, on the Great North Road, and at Digswell Water on the Hertford Road, as well as at each of the hamlets.

Law and Order

In feudal times law and order – and punishment – had been the responsibility of individual manors. Because the rector of Welwyn was lord of the manor he is said to have had gallows by the church! Rectors held manorial courts (as well as vestries) until a century ago. Hatfield manor had stocks in the churchyard, and a lock-up still survived in Church Street in 1838.

A Saxon system of 'tithing' adult men into groups of ten, each answerable for the good behaviour of the rest, persisted well into the 15th century. A slow and haphazard transition from manorial to parish administration followed the social upheaval caused by the mid-14th-century Black Death. Ludwickhyde, 'Woodsyd' and Hatfield appointed constables in the 16th century, Welwyn Rectory Manor did so until 1636, and Digswell to 1644. Parishes, rather than manors, appointed constables from the mid-17th century.

Elected local constables were frequently ineffective, and from the late 18th century local Residents Associations offered rewards for convictions; Hatfield's association dated from 1807. Eventually some employed their own police. The County Police Act of 1839 enabled JPs to appoint

66 Church House, Welwyn on a postcard sent in 1920, at which time it was the police station.

67 The first Garden City police station in Stonehills, 1936.

68 One of the glass gaming pieces from the 'Panshanger' Belgic chieftain burial.

forces, and the Hertfordshire force dates from 1841. The county headquarters was established in Goldrings (or Goldings or Golby) at Hatfield. It moved into purpose-built premises in 1883, and transferred to Stanborough in 1967. Welwyn station moved from Church House to 31 Church Street at the beginning of the 20th century, and thence to the Garden City in 1933. A small, part-time sub-station was also built in the 1950s, attached to police houses in School Lane. There were four constables in Welwyn Garden City in the 1920s, but the police station had to wait until 1933. It was on the west side of Stonehills ('Project D'). In 1962 a new police station was opened on the Campus and the old building was demolished.

From the 14th century feudal lords had been appointed as county magistrates but by the 17th century the posts were filled by local 'squires'. The Welwyn Justices of the Peace met at the *White Hart* but moved to Hatfield in 1904. Hatfield cases were heard in Hertford until 1893; thereafter the court was in the *Salisbury Arms* until 1900, and then the police station until the Mid-Herts County Court, St Albans Road opened in 1939. In 1998 it transferred to a new Central Herts. Bench at St Albans.

Country Pursuits
A rural area with two rivers was never without hunting, hawking, shooting and fishing. The lords

of Digswell had the right of warren (small animals of the chase) in the 12th century. The 1599 map of the manor shows a warren, with rabbits, and a man with a gun, at Black Fan. In addition to the ancient deer park at Hatfield there were others at Woodhall and Brocket, and the Queen kept greyhounds for hare coursing. Otter and fox hounds were kept at Hatfield in the early 17th century, and public packs were hunting in the area by the eighteenth. Horses were trained at Brocket for steeplechasing, where there was a racecourse at the beginning of the 19th century. Records from game books and other sources suggest there was an abundance and that almost anything was fair game. In a wager, Cuyler of Danesbury shot 24 brace of partridge in one-and-a-half hours at Hatfield. Trout were fished with dry fly, and there was also plenty of coarse fish. James I kept cormorants at Hatfield.

Archaeological discoveries have unearthed less aristocratic pursuits. There were glass gaming counters in the Belgic chieftain's burial at Grubs Barn, for example, but the board had rotted. Roman dice and counters have also been found, but such pastimes leave little evidence. Games which were banned under Henry VIII included shovegroat, tables, dice, tennis, bowles, closh (nine-pins), coytes and logettes.

Early field sports were played on improvised pitches. There was a bowling alley behind the Assembly Rooms at Welwyn in the late 18th century, for example. Archery practice was

By DESIRE of the

Rev. Mr. ROUSE

Positively the LAST Night.

THEATRE, WELWYN

On FRIDAY Evening, the 13th of JUNE, 1794.

Will be prefented, a favorite COMEDY call'd

Every One has his Fault.

Irwin,   Mr.   MELVILLE
Lord Moreland,   Mr.   HARDING
Mr. Harmony,   Mr.   FRIMBLY
Edward,   Mifs   CRISP
Servant,   Mr.   CRISP
And, Sir Robert Ramble, Mr.   CRISP, Jun.
Mifs Woobourn,   Mifs   GROVES
Mrs. Placid,   Mrs. BAKEWELL
And, Lady Eleanor Irwin,   Mrs.   CRISP.

Singing by Mafter and Mifs CRISP, and Mifs GROVES.

To which will be added, a MUSICAL ENTERTAINMENT call'd

The ROMP.

Old Barnacle,   Mr.   FRIMBLY
Captain Sightly,   Mr.   MELVILLE
Old Cockney,   Mr.   HARDING
Servant,   Mafter   CRISP
And, Watty Cockney, Mr. CRISP, Jun.
Mifs La Blond,   Mrs.   CRISP
Penelope,   Mrs. BAKEWELL
Quafheba,   Mifs   CRISP
And, Prifcilla Tomboy, (the Romp)   Mifs   GROVES.

BOXES, 3s.---PIT, 2s----GALLERY, 1s.

TICKETS to be had of Mr CRISP

69   An 18th-century playbill.

once required by statute and cricket was deplored as a competitor, but by 1749 there was a Hertfordshire cricket team; the Otways of Welwyn were members in the early 19th century and R.D. Balfour of 'Sherrards' went in to bat with W.G. Grace when MCC played Hertfordshire in 1872. The late 18th-century Carrington Diaries mention matches at Tewin Upper Green. Some were 'single wicket' matches played for wagers between named individuals, or between scratch teams, such as married men and bachelors, but each village and many hamlets had teams too; the pitches were on village greens or provided by the gentry in their parks, by Shee at Lockleys Warren, the Cowpers at Digswell, or the Blakes at Welwyn. In 1928 there were two cricket grounds in the Garden City.

Danesbury and Marden Hill had private golf-courses in the 19th century. A nine-hole club course was opened at Welwyn Garden City in 1923, which was enlarged to 18 holes in 1930. A public 'Panshanger' course was opened in the north-east in 1975. Other club courses have been opened at Chequers and at Danesbury.

The local place-name 'Sticky Court' is evidence that real tennis 'sphairistke' was played at Digswell House and by the early years of the 20th century many private houses had croquet lawns and tennis courts. Tennis, like golf, was a fashionable middle-class game and it is revealing how many tennis courts are shown on the west side of the railway in early maps of the Garden City. In 1928 there were 12 hard courts.

Although football is mentioned in early records, games between organised teams with formal rules seem to be a late 19th-century innovation. Dagmar House Old Boys Football Club was founded at Hatfield in 1900 and amalgamated with Hatfield Football Club in about 1906. In 1908 Welwyn won the Hertfordshire Junior League.

Clubs and Assemblies

The 18th century was the period when spas became fashionable and Dr. Young attempted to establish one based on the chalybeate spring at Welwyn. Although the project failed, Assembly Rooms were built which contained a theatre. They are still standing in Mill Lane, converted to cottages.

Many kinds of social gathering in the past were held in public houses. There was a Smoking Club at *The Swan*, Welwyn in the late 18th century, and a Friendly Club (for social security) at *The Vine* shortly after. A Social Club of more universal membership was established in Welwyn in January 1876, which met for many years in 'rooms' in the *White Hart* and organised outings. The committee was entirely male and the rector was president. The *Parish Magazine* in the late 19th century gives details of a parish library and a Welcome Reading Room in a house provided by C.W. Wilshere of The Frythe. A Boys Club met in the 1880s in Becket Hall, built by W.W. Wilshere for the use of the parish and as a drill hall.

A resolution that a village hall be built and operated by a limited company is recorded in the *Parish*

Magazine in 1867 but it is not until 1877 that the rector writes that he has purchased an iron [corrugated] room. The sum of £340 10s. was raised and St Mary's Hall was erected and fitted out beside the Manor House gates in School Lane. It was demolished in 1966 after the Civic Centre, which incorporated a county branch library and welfare clinic, had been opened by the Rural District Council at Prospect Place.

Early Schools
A school with four children is recorded at Welwyn in 1714. It was still there in 1720, probably in Church House, and in 1739 Dr. Young rented Anchor Pightle, behind the *Rose and Crown* (now part of the churchyard), as a playground and a purpose-built school was there by 1755. Five years later Young established it as a proper foundation for 16 pupils. It moved to a National School in School Lane before 1830.

Several private schools were established at Welwyn. William Otway's was at the Old Rectory from the end of the 18th century until his death in 1838, when his own children continued the work until about 1840: John at the Old Rectory

70   Title page of the rule-book of the New Union Society, Welwyn.

71   Dr. Edward Young's first school in Anchor Pightle, now the north-east extension of Welwyn churchyard.

LAWS,

RULES AND ORDERS,

TO BE OBSERVED

BY THE

NEW UNION SOCIETY,

AT THE

VINE INN,

IN

WELLWYN,

HERTFORDSHIRE.

Begun the 1st Monday in November, 1793.

HERTFORD:

PRINTED BY ST. AUSTIN,

1813.

THE LAST DAY — FEBRUARY 15th 1985

72 'The Last Day – February 15th 1985'. This picture, painted by the late Kate Rook to record the final playtime, hangs on walls all over the world.

(boys) and Eliza at East End House, or Parkside (girls). In 1826 Thomas Fox kept a preparatory school at Ivy Cottage (beside *The Wellington*) which continued as a school until 1900, when it was run by Miss Applegarth. An assistant there in 1876 was Anne, sister of Vincent Van Gogh, who visited Welwyn to see her. The 1833 Education Return records four infant schools at Welwyn, with 24 boys and 39 girls. There were three daily schools; one, supported in part by the rector's wife, had 35 girl pupils, and contained a lending library; another had 25 boys, and the third, which started that year, had 13 boys and 26 girls. Two boarding schools had 18 girl pupils, and the National and Sunday school 70 boys; it 'had a small endowment', and contained a lending library. All the schools charged for tuition.

In the middle of the 19th century, the Rev. Thomas Rowe of the Independent Chapel ran a school, and the Rev. John Tuck, curate of Ayot St

Peter, another, with 12 boarders aged between seven and 15 years. At Parkside a School for Ladies was kept by Mr. and Mrs. Raves in 1886. St Patrick's, a boys' school, was run at The Grange by the Rev. W.H. Wynne in 1922, and after 1926 it was run as a kindergarten by his wife. A.V. Miller kept a boarding and preparatory school, called The Grange School, from 1929 until his retirement in 1968, when it closed. It took boarders as young as six years old.

Welwyn St Mary's Primary School at the top of Welwyn Hill opened in 1858 with 90 boys, 70 girls and 60 infants, and in 1940 the new senior school was opened behind it. This retained the 'allotment gardens' designed for those pupils who did not move on to secondary education. The infants moved into this school with the junior pupils in 1983 and the senior pupils were transferred to Monks Walk comprehensive. The 19th-century school became part of a sheltered housing development in 1986. Oaklands Nursery School, originally opposite the

North Star, moved into a new Tenterfield Nursery School which was opened in 1965.

At Hatfield, Robert Clough was licensed to teach in 1596, but the location of his establishment is unknown. The first recorded school was for forty girls, founded by Countess Anne in 1739, and in 1746 there is a record of two well-endowed charity schools. In 1760 Eliazer (*sic*) Burchell ran a boarding school in the churchyard. By 1839 James Austin was 'Master of the National School', possibly in the Market House, which transferred to Puttocks Oak in 1842 when the Market House was demolished. The Rev. F.J. Faithful taught at the Vicarage and Parsonage from 1812 to 1828 and built a girls' school at about this time. Benjamin Peile ran a school at Puttocks Oak in 1838; he moved to Northcutts in 1839 but the school closed in 1860. In 1839 Mark Powell ran a school in Fore Street and Thomas Smith ran a Writing School in North Road. In 1851 Sarah Chapman had a school in Back Street and the Rev. Thomas Ray (an Independent minister) taught 17 boys in Fore Street. From 1862 there was a young gentlemen's boarding school in 'The Triangular House'. In 1871 it moved to Dagmar House, where it continued until 1934. Miss C.S. Dare's ladies' school, founded in Morton House, Fore Street in 1886, moved to Dagmar House in 1898, to the adjacent Alexandra House in 1900, and closed in 1934.

In 1850 a London Road National School opened in Hare's Maltings. The boys moved to a new building at the corner of Endymion Road and School Lane in 1905 but the girls and infants stayed in the old building; the infants were moved to Countess Anne's in 1913. The girls remained in a building described in 1924 as 'out-of-date, unhygienic, unhealthy and insufficient'. A senior and junior mixed school, St Audrey's, was opened in 1939, and destroyed by a V1 or 'Doodlebug' flying bomb in 1944. A new secondary modern school was provided in 1946. In 1957 a new school, no longer a church school, opened in Travellers Lane.

In his will dated May 1773, Henry Yarborough DD gave all his houses and real estate in Tewin for the maintenance of a parish clerk and a schoolmaster to teach ten poor children of the parish, and in 1783 Elizabeth, Lady Cathcart gave East India annuities to provide coal for the school. The Cowper Endowed

73 Roman hematite amulet found at Dicket Mead Villa, Welwyn. It calls upon supernatural Egyptian, Greek and Hebrew beings to protect the wearer in childbirth.

School was built under the will of Henry Cowper who died in 1838. In 1833 Digswell had a daily school with seven boys and 27 girls, Ayot St Peter an infants' school with 30 children, and at Lemsford there was already a Dame School with about 40 pupils when Earl Cowper built the primary school in 1872. A school was held 'in the mud chapel' at Hatfield Hyde church from 1861. A new school for 56 infants and juniors was built by Lord Salisbury in 1875, which closed in 1932 and was demolished in 1950. In 1872 Cowper's Church of England school was opened at Lemsford.

Health and Hygiene

The earliest local evidence for medicine is probably a magical amulet, intended to protect a woman in childbirth, which was found by the author at Dicket Mead Roman villa. There would have been 'leeches', herbalists, and doctors throughout time but they are largely unchronicled. Many of the cures relied on faith or magic rather than science;

74 Certificate of 1683 allowing Ann Harper of Welwyn to be touched for the King's Evil.

a certificate of 1683 states that 'Ann Harper of the parish of Welwyn in Hertfordshire, supposed to be troubled by the disease commonly called King's Evil hath not … at any time been touched by the King's Majesty with intent to be healed of that disease.' John Twydell, clerk to the Welwyn Vestry, was paid 11s. 8d. 'for one years writing for the year 1709 and a bill for the cure of Mary Smith's fingers'. In 1851 there were two doctors and a surgeon in Welwyn. A Married Women's Club was formed in 1877. The subscription of five shillings, paid in instalments during the six months before confinement gave attendance of midwife and 'if necessary a medical man'.

Not until the 19th century was there scientific evidence of a connection between hygiene and health. Even then, action was slow. At Welwyn in 1848 'the question of draining the town was brought before the vestry'. It is not clear what was done then but a 'new' drainage system was installed in 1872. However, in 1875 the district Medical Officer wrote, 'The bed of the river between the bridge and the mill is very offensive when the mud, which has not been cleaned out since sewage was deposited there, is exposed.' He added a year later, 'The greatest need is a more plentiful supply of fresh water for domestic use,' and advocated storing rain water. In June 1878 he pointed out that the burial registers indicated that, since 1558, 'bodies buried in the churchyard must be three deep in all but 10 graves'. Because of the contamination of wells, a new cemetery, distant from the village, was consecrated in 1882.

At Hatfield in 1868 Lord Salisbury's agent ignored notices threatening action because cottages his lordship owned had privies which drained into the River Lea at Lemsford. Many houses in the town were 'without privy accommodation of any kind'. The situation here was worsened because the river did not flow past the houses. An open watercourse, 'The Black Ditch', ran alongside the boundary of the park, beside the Hertford Road opposite The Ryde, to Mill Green. In 1868 it was noted that, 'The sewage is turned out onto the Hertford Road from the Black Ditch to enable Mr. Webb to clean out the wells and lengthen the tunnel … and what is got out during the day is covered with lime. The stench is certainly very bad and with the wind blowing in the direction of the town, very injurious to health.' In August 1869 J.W. Knight, the owner of Bush Hall, wrote 'I have now to inform you that within a few hundred yards of my house and directly opposite Mill Green there is a large pond of sewage conveyed there by means of an open ditch from Hatfield; the stench is intolerable.'

In October of that year land was purchased from Lord Salisbury for a sewerage scheme which involved pipe laying and the construction of settling tanks, which were, at the later insistence of his lordship, covered. Details of the scheme are not known, since when the work was inspected in 1907 with a view to improvement no plans or sections were found. Piped water was being pumped from a deep well at Rose Green, and also obtained from a spring in the park. Rainwater and foul water were not being separated, the fall on the pipe was insufficient, and the settling tanks were never cleaned

75 An obsolete sewage pumping station in Orchard Road, originally built by Welwyn Rural District Council.

out. As a consequence, raw sewage escaped from the irrigation area on Billet Common straight into the Lea, from which The New River extracted water at Hertford to supply London. The resulting improvements included a pump which was installed at Mill Green and a sewage farm built higher on the Common.

A sewage farm was constructed at Welwyn in 1868 on land east of the old Assembly Rooms, and mains water was supplied to the village from the pumping station in School Lane by the beginning of the 20th century. In 1922 a pump-house was built which pumped the waste to a sewage farm destroyed when the motorway was built in 1969. By this time Welwyn was connected to the Mimram valley main sewer.

Water supply and drainage were of primary importance for the new Garden City. The existing well in Handside was deepened and pumps installed,

and a new pumping station was built below Digswell Park in 1923. Surface water drains were laid to the rivers, and a sewage farm constructed to the east of Black Fan. The undertaking was sold to the Urban District Council in 1932. Later development made use of the Hatfield sewage works. The existing system was insufficient for the intended population of the New Town and the sewage system was connected to Rye Meads via the trunk sewer in 1958. In 1961 the Lee Valley Water Co. took over from the Urban District Council. The undertaking is now run by Three Rivers.

There was a 'pest house' for the isolation of smallpox sufferers before 1761, and a new one was opened in Ninnings Wood in 1774. In 1901-2 the Queen Victoria Memorial Hospital for Welwyn, Codicote, Digswell and Knebworth was built by voluntary subscription beside the Codicote Road; the building is now a private dwelling. The Trustees

76 The first Queen
Victoria Memorial
Hospital, Codicote Road,
Welwyn pictured on a
postcard sent in 1912.

included Earl Cowper, A.M. Blake of Danesbury
and the rector. Patients or their friends paid a
maximum of 10s. 6d., 'the amount to be determined by the committee'. It is interesting to read
that admission was not permitted to maternity cases,
epilepsy, diphtheria, incurable malady or contagious
or infectious diseases.

Public Utilities

For most of man's history, meagre domestic illumi-
nation was obtained from lighting wicks soaked in
oil or fat. The first mention of street lighting, the
oil lamps provided in Welwyn by the vestry and
the Turnpike Trust, is not until 1820. In 1860 a
gasworks was built at Hatfield by a private company

77 Welwyn Vestry
minutes, showing
payment made to a
watchman after a fire in
1661.

78   The disastrous fire at Danesbury in September 1920.

which intended, but could not afford, the installa-
tion of street lighting in the town. At Welwyn, in
the same year, George Dering of Lockleys built a
gasworks in a gravel pit on the south side of the
Hertford Road opposite the *White Hart*, and shortly
afterwards gas lamps were lit from Michaelmas to
Lady Day, and paid for by public subscription, which
was not always forthcoming. In 1874 the *Parish
Magazine* records that 'last winter our streets were
left in darkness every night because there was not
enough public spirit … to defray the cost'. The
gasworks were leased to a private individual, became
the Welwyn Knebworth Gas Co. in 1912 and part
of the Welwyn Hatfield Gas Co. in 1913. Gas was
supplied by this company to Welwyn Garden City
in 1921; gasholders, and eventually a gasworks, were
built beside Tewin Road and Tewin Wood was
provided with gas in 1925. Welwyn and Hatfield
Gasworks were demolished after the Welwyn & St
Albans Co. was formed in 1933.

An undated hook on a long pole, used for
removing burning thatch from roofs, hung beneath
the jetty of Church House in Welwyn and was the
earliest form of fire prevention. A fire engine was

being provided in Welwyn before 1761, when the
churchwardens were ordered by the vestry to keep
'the Engine' and 'the Buckets' in useful repair.

In 1807 John Carrington records a man passing
him on the Great North Road 'for the Welwyn
engine' to fight a fire at Stevenage, and the 1820
account for its repair survives. In 1873 up to £100
was voted to improve the engine for the volunteer
brigade. The fire station moved about 1880 to a
site between The Steamer and Becket Hall. Manual
pumps were still in use, and the private brigade at
Tewin Water estate, which had a steam pump, an
escape and a hose cart, gave protection to the surrounding villages. At Welwyn manual pumps were
used when Danesbury was virtually destroyed by
fire in 1920. In 1938 the brigade was taken over
by the Rural District Council and the fire station
at Prospect Place was opened. After the war it was
adopted by the County, which enlarged it in 1998.

Hatfield brigade was started in 1881, and a fire
station was built in Batterdale in 1899. A horse-
drawn steam pump was in use in 1909. New
premises were provided in Wellfield Road and the
old station demolished in 1966.

79   The old Fire Station at Hatfield.

The infant Garden City was in the area served by the Hatfield brigade with back-up from those at Welwyn and the Tewin Water estate. In 1922 thirty feet of hose on a handcart was stored in a hut on Bridge Road for use by the volunteer brigade. In 1929 an engine and equipment were purchased by the Urban District Council. A full-time brigade of 12 men moved into a fire station with hose tower built as an integral part of the Council Offices. This became a County responsibility in 1938. Larger quarters were provided in Bridge Road East in 1978.

Church and Chapel

Several nonconformist places of worship were created in the area of study. John Bunyan is said to have preached in a barn, now the Barn Theatre. A Wesleyan Chapel was built in 1822 at Ayot Green, and the site of another in Lemsford is now part of the car park of the *Long Arm and Short Arm*. The Bethel Independent Chapel had been opened in 1792 on Hobbs Hill, Welwyn but the building became a private house when a new

chapel was built in Fulling Mill Lane in 1955. This became an Evangelical Church, which was replaced with a new building on the same site in 1959, and then extended in 1968. A breakaway sect built themselves a chapel in Mimram Walk in 1834, which became the Ebenezer Strict Baptist Chapel in 1885.

There was a Baptist Chapel in Park Street, Hatfield from 1823 to 1932, when Christ Church in St Albans Road was opened. The Wesleyan congregation met in several places until they settled in 'The Moo-cow Chapel' (an aromatic agricultural building) at the top of Church Street in about 1851. In 1899 they moved to a new church in French Horn Lane. This was closed in 1938, when they transferred to Birchwood Avenue. A Roman Catholic church was established on the site of the Carmelite Convent (now demolished) in 1930; the circular Marychurch was built in 1970.

Several Acts of Parliament in the reign of Victoria, such as that in 1843 'to make better Provision for the Spiritual Care of populous Parishes', made it possible for new parishes to be created and churches

80 Park Street Baptist Chapel, Hatfield.

81 Rear of St Mary Magdalene's, Hatfield Hyde, before its enlargement in 1957.

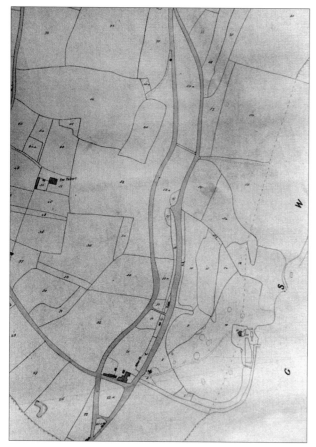

82 Detail from the Welwyn Tithe Map of 1837 showing the older Mountain Slough still in use beside McAdam's turnpike. This would have functioned as a drove road until the railway opened.

to be built in rural areas where the parish church was a long way away, such as northern Hatfield. Lemsford Parish was approved by the Queen in Council in 1858; the Church of St John, in Early English gothic, was dedicated the following year. In 1930 the chancel was extended and an extraordinary Perpendicular-style chapel added at the southeast corner.

At Hatfield Hyde, a 'chapel of ease' dedicated to St Mary Magdalene, was built in 1883 to replace an earlier structure called 'the mud chapel', built in 1861. It was served by a curate from Hatfield. During the week the chancel was curtained off and the nave was used as a school and a public hall. Hatfield Hyde became a parish, with Peartree, in 1927; the church was enlarged in 1957.

An Anglican Mission chapel, dedicated to King Charles the Martyr, was built by William Wilshere of The Frythe at Harmer Green in 1881; it was converted into a private house in 1970. A church was opened for the Pentecostal Assembly in Hyde Valley in 1955. The Methodist Church held its first services in the Community Centre in 1944. The church in Ludwick Way was opened in 1957. A new Methodist church was opened in Warren Way, Digswell in 1964.

Roads and Rail

In 1834 McAdam's improvements to the road, which included the introduction of 'macadamizing' – the use of small stones to form the surface of roads – by-passed Lemsford via Stanborough (New Road) and re-routed Mountain Slough (below Digswell Place) onto the side of the valley into Welwyn. By the early 19th century one of the coaching inns in Welwyn was said to provide horses for 'upwards of eighty coaches per day'. Main roads were improved piecemeal. Fore Street in Hatfield was extended, and the difficult turns through Lizard Lane eliminated by the creation of Brewery Hill. A notable oddity was the turnpike road which ran from Hatfield through St Albans and Watford; the milestones which survive along it give distances to Reading. It was nicknamed 'The Gout Track' because it enabled Lord Salisbury and the Earl of Essex (who lived at Cassiobury) to travel comfortably to Bath to 'take the waters'.

The coming of the Great Northern Railway rendered the local turnpike trust no longer viable and it was dissolved in 1862. Main roads became the responsibility of Highway Boards and were maintained out of County funds. The County Council took responsibility after its foundation in 1888. Shortly after the turn of the century the use of coal tar to alleviate the dust which pneumatic tyres sucked from between the stones led to the invention of 'tarmac'.

The Main Line Railway

Because railways required very shallow gradients, their builders, like the prehistoric makers of the earliest trackways, endeavoured to follow the river valleys. A line was projected for the Great Northern

83   The Great North Road south of Valley Road Corner, pictured on a postcard sent in 1913. The buildings are Cowper estate cottages.

84   Nearing Digswell on the Great North Road, *c.*1904.

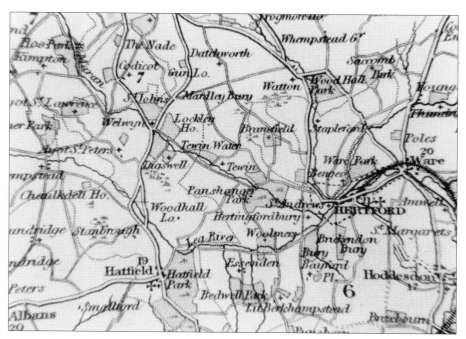

85 Dugdale's map of about 1840 indicates parkland with shading, although Brocket has not been shaded and Tewin was a park but there was no house. The new railway threaded between Digswell and Tewin Water.

Railway up the Mimram valley, but most of the proposed route was owned and landscaped by riparian estate owners. Opposition from these, especially, it is said, from Lord Dacre of The Hoo at Whitwell, dictated an extraordinary route which, in 1851, threaded between Digswell Park, Lockleys Park and Tewin Water, over a mile from Welwyn town, crossing the valley on Digswell Viaduct and

plunging into a tunnel at its north end. The site of a small settlement, Cobble (or Cob Lane) End, marked on early maps is now under the north abutment of the viaduct; Cob Lane Common still exists by Welwyn North Station, which was constructed at this time.

By now Welwyn had become the *de facto* economic and administrative centre of a large area

86   Welwyn Viaduct from the *Illustrated London News*, August 1850.

87 Blow's beehive works seen fom the railway, *c.*1898. The site is now Honeymead, near Welwyn North station.

of mid-Hertfordshire, with momentum adequate to survive the consequent loss of the coaching trade. Under the 1894 Local Government Act the vestry gave place to the civil Parish Council as the administrative body for the villages. Welwyn was joined with Digswell, Ayot St Peter and Ayot St Law-rence in one of the smallest Rural District Councils in the country.

Unlike the landowners along the Mimram valley, Lord Salisbury positively encouraged the railway company, and exploited it. It paid £8,000 towards the rerouting of the Great North Road away from

88 Lord Salisbury's private waiting room at Hatfield station shortly before it was demolished.

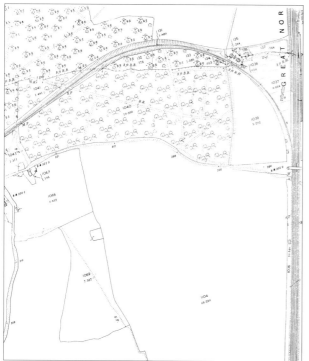

the park and straight into the town, and also built him a private waiting room, a VIP lounge where he could welcome and bid farewell to his guests. During parliamentary sessions he had his own crack express at Hatfield, under steam at all times, to take him as necessary to the House.

The Great Northern Railway did not at first encourage commuters, and Lockleys estate effectively prevented extension or migration of Welwyn village towards the station. It was not until the beginning of the 20th century that High Welwyn Limited created New Road, and houses were already being built there when Howard bought the land for the Garden City.

The main line was electrified by an overhead gantry system in 1974. New sidings for out-of-

89 Ordnance Survey map of Welwyn Garden City town centre area in 1898.

90 Welwyn Garden City railway station was on the Luton branch prior to 1923.

91   Welwyn Garden City railway station shortly before its official opening in October 1926.

service rolling stock were constructed east of the Campus and a high-level cross-over enabled trains to terminate at Welwyn Garden City 'down' platform and return to the City on the 'up' line when the Moorgate service opened in 1976.

The Branch Lines

Plans for a continuous railway across the county from Hertford to Dunstable and Luton came to grief when the Great Northern refused to allow the line to cross its metals. A temporary, oddly named 'Welwyn' station was therefore built in open country when the Hertford branch was completed in 1853. This was demolished in 1860 and the Hertford and Luton branches were connected to the main line and then served by Hatfield station. It seems likely that the potential of 'Welwyn' junction (it was actually close to the parish boundary between Digswell and Hatfield) attracted the eye of the planners of the 'Second Garden City' and influenced the eventual choice of its name.

A station was opened at Ayot St Peter on the Dunstable line in about 1878 and at Attimore Halt on the Hertford branch in 1905. Horn's sidings, now the site of Campus West car park, served the local farms run by the Horn family and, eventually, the Garden City builders. In October 1920 a small

station was built nearby to serve Welwyn Garden City. Passengers had to change at Hatfield for the main line or for Hertford until a station was opened on the present site in 1926. This would be remodelled in 1990 when the Howard Centre was built.

The Hertford branch was closed for passengers in 1951 and the Dunstable branch in 1963. Both lines continued in use. However, to the east and west of the Garden City site were large gravel pits to which domestic refuse was taken as land-fill. The waste was processed at a rail-side works in Lower Holloway (near the Arsenal football ground), where tins and holloware were removed, and was then taken by rail to Blackbridge Pits, near Ayot St Lawrence (to the annoyance of George Bernard Shaw) and to Cole Green Pit. In 1937, 77,000 tons were sent from Islington; in 1939 Stoke Newington refuse was added, giving 83,000 tons. With Hackney also contributing by now, the total in 1947 was 110,000 tons. The refuse trains continued to use the branch lines until 1965, and after that the Hertford branch was used as a goods line for the industrial area as far as the Attimore (Ridgeway) crossing until the early 1980s.

Another branch of the Great Northern Railway was constructed from Hatfield to St Albans in 1862. The general goods service ended in 1964 and the

92   The rail crash in Welwyn tunnel in June 1866. It is unlikely the artist had seen the real thing.

line was closed in 1968. Prior to the development of Welwyn Garden City, Hatfield was effectively the junction for all three branches from the main line to St Albans, Luton and Hertford: a railway town with its own engine sheds.

Just over six weeks after Hatfield station was opened a collision in the station seriously injured seven people. The first spectacular local rail accident occurred when three trains collided in Welwyn tunnel in June 1866. Two men died and the wreckage was allowed to burn itself out. A train

was derailed at Ayot in May 1926. In June 1935 the Leeds mail train crashed into the Newcastle express as the latter was accelerating at Welwyn Garden City station having been slowed by a signalling error; 14 people died and, as a result of recommendations by the enquiry, the signalling system on all railways was changed. In January 1957 the Aberdeen to Kings Cross express struck a local train and was derailed just south of Twentieth Mile Bridge; there was one fatality.

Seven

The Company

The First Plans

When Norman Savill, who had bid for the land Howard bought, discovered that the old man had insufficient money even to pay the ten per cent deposit, he made him an advance out of his own money! Howard borrowed another few thousand pounds and offered Frederic Osborn £8 a week to organise the new project and form a company. Part of Osborn's first week's pay was spent on equipment and materials to produce an outline 'Theoretical Layout: without regard to contours'. Dated 18 June 1919, it echoes the concentric form of Howard's diagrams. It included land belonging to the Marquess of Salisbury, which Osborn thought was essential to the project. He wrote in July making a firm offer for 1,019 acres at, or near, Hatfield Hyde. Lengthy negotiations resulted in the purchase in October of 694 acres for £40,000, with the proviso that it would be sold back if the scheme failed. There was insufficient land for the agricultural belt, and Lord Desborough was approached for a further 250 acres of Panshanger estate. He was, however, opposed to the project.

The Second Garden City Company

The Second Garden City Limited was floated in October 1919. Howard, Osborn, Purdom and Reiss recruited a provisional board which produced a memorandum, 'The Proposed Second Garden City near Welwyn, Herts.', on 1 July 1919. In April 1920 another company, Welwyn Garden City Ltd., succeeded it with authorised capital of £250,000 in £1 shares. No more than seven per cent would be paid in dividends and any surplus would be used for the benefit of the town and its inhabitants. All land would be copyhold, on a 999-year lease. The Second Garden City Company was itself one

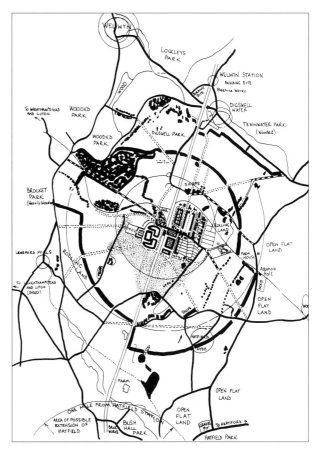

93 Frederic Osborn's sketch map of the Garden City (re-drawn from a dye-line print).

of the principal shareholders, being given a holding of 12,659 shares, but doing no business. This was a foretaste of future labyrinthine business dealings.

The board was strengthened, and Sir Theodore Chambers, a Freemason, professional surveyor and company director who had been Controller of National Savings during the war, joined in

71

94 F. Osborn and T. Chambers walking on the newly purchased site in 1919.

95 The book produced by the New Towns Trust.

November. He 'had a Rolls Royce outlook compared with the ... tin-Lizzie aspirations to which we Letchworthians had been conditioned' wrote Osborn, and insisted on employing experts. He held the post of chairman of Welwyn Garden City Ltd. until the town was taken over by the Development Corporation in 1948, and continued to be chairman of its successor, Howardsgate Trust, until his resignation after 33 years' service, in May 1954, at the age of eighty-three. He died three years later.

The New Towns Trust
At the end of the First World War a group drawn mainly from members of the Society of Friends (Quakers) had formed the New Towns Trust with the intention of building their own town, to be run on the principles set out in a book by W.R. Hughes called *New Town*. Hughes' ideals differed

from Howard's, inasmuch as he emphasised the spiritual welfare and education of people more than their physical well-being, the material inequalities of society, or land reform. Their proposed town was to be based mainly on agriculture and craft industries, and was reminiscent of the Arts and Crafts Movement. The Trust had been seeking a suitable site with a minimum of 18,000 acres (compared with the initial purchase for Welwyn Garden City of 1,688 acres including Sherrardspark Wood, 2,382 acres with the Salisbury land) 'within the area of a local authority with enlightened methods and practice of local government'. It had examined, often on the ground, the merits of nearly seventy estates in an area defined by London, Bristol, Liverpool and York, plus East Anglia, and agreed that 'some features of the scheme as outlined in the book "New Town" will probably be sacrificed'.

96   An undated picture of the Company's Electricity works in Bridge Road East.

After some disagreement with Welwyn Garden City Ltd. over the status of industry and education, the New Towns Trust, with changed rules and renamed Welwyn Pioneer Trust, which offered a maximum six per cent return to its investors, signed an agreement with the Company in February 1921. Under the terms of this agreement the Trust were to nominate a representative to the Board of the Garden City Company, but the cooperation was 'gravely prejudiced' when the Trust's General Manager was not accepted on the Board 'as his position as a member of the Trust and of a subsidiary of both organisations would be prejudicial to both his position as officer and director'. In other words, he might know too much of what went on behind closed doors!

The Trust was then shocked to find that, although the Company offered a maximum dividend of only seven per cent to its investors, 'to ensure the issue of capital should retain its character as an undertaking conducted in the public interest', this limitation did not apply to its subsidiaries, whose almost byzantine relationship to the parent company is today impossible to unravel. Debts, as well as one another's stocks and shares, material assets, and property were shuffled about between them, often at book values. Anything that needed doing, it seems, was in the hands of the Company, from construction (Welwyn Buildings and Joiners Ltd.), Brickmaking (Welwyn Brick Works Ltd.), to trees and shrubs (Welwyn Nurseries Ltd.), to retailing (Welwyn Stores Ltd.). The cinema was run by Welwyn Theatres Ltd. and the light railway by Welwyn Transport Ltd., who also ran a fleet of vehicles for other subsidiary companies and sold coal and petrol.

97 One of the Company's steam waggons making a delivery in London.

98 An early view of the west front of the Company's laundry in Broadwater Road, seen from Bridge Road East. These buildings were demolished in 2000.

The Agricultural Guild

The Welwyn Pioneer Trust formed an agricultural sub-committee and bought Lower Handside Farm, then became the Agricultural Guild, which progressively took over the tenancies of up to 1,650 acres of Company farmland, including, when they became available in 1924, Stanborough and some of the farms on the Salisbury estate, including Woodhall. The farms were managed by a committee, with Heads of Departments (including Mr. Horn), four farm workers, a representative of the farmworkers' union and two representatives of the New Towns Trust. The mixed farming included market gardening with greenhouses, and an orchard planted at Brickwall. The Guild's pigs were celebrated, and its milk, both certified (TT) and uncertified, supplied Welwyn Stores and the London Hospital for Diseases of the Heart and Lungs. Welwyn Stores Ltd., to which the Trust's Agricultural Guild was to supply produce, was a monopoly, no other retailers being permitted. It

99   Stanborough Farm.

offered a dividend up to 15 per cent, and insisted that suppliers kept wholesale prices secret.

Either because of the state of agriculture at the time, or the management by idealistic amateurs, or both, the Guild ran at a loss which the Trust had little income to offset. The Trust took it over in

100   Woodhall Lodge Farm was demolished in 1958 when Chequers was built.

101 Brickwall Farmhouse was demolished in 2000.

102 Arrival of an early Garden City resident: Molly Jenkins with her caravan on the Great North Road.

August 1925, sacking and re-employing the staff without loss of service. A year later the Trust itself was swallowed up by the Garden City Company. Milk production was taken over by yet another subsidiary of Welwyn Garden City Limited, Welwyn Dairies Ltd., and the undeveloped farmland was re-let to independent holders in small parcels.

Newspapers

At first there were two local weekly newspapers, *Welwyn Garden City News*, run by Welwyn Publications Ltd., another subsidiary of the Company (for nine years the front page was an advertisement for Welwyn Stores), and *The Pilot*, which openly criticised the Company and its subsidiaries. In 1928 Mr. and Mrs. Sault, the owners of *The Pilot*, were offered £500 cash, £750 in preference shares and

103   Nos 34-8 Parkway during construction.

£750 ordinary shares in a new publication, the *Welwyn Times*, which would replace the *News*, to sign a covenant not to publish any newspaper in the area, nor to allow the title of *The Pilot* to be used for any other local paper. In addition, litigation by Sault against one of the Company's directors would cease on consideration of a further payment of costs of £100. Action by Welwyn Publications against Sault (it was alleged that he had published a local directory in breach of their copyright) had already been dropped on Counsel's advice. The *Welwyn Times*, nominally independent, was nevertheless one of the Company's subsidiaries, with three of its directors on the Board. 'We are not publishing a newspaper … We are helping build a city', said the editorial of its first edition – which inevitably devoted the whole of its front page to advertising Welwyn Stores.

Money Raising

Without development there would be no income. With no houses there would be no industrial workforce and with no factories there would be nowhere to work, except with the developers. The Company created 20,000 six-per-cent 40-year debentures at £50 – which were not advertised; the directors were 'prepared to allocate shareholders and friends on application by letter'. Luckily, under new legislation, government loans became available. £117,000 was borrowed from the Public Loans Commission at five per cent. 'The issue of the balance of £150,000 debenture will permit application for a further £148,000.'

In 1921 Welwyn Builders undertook the construction of 110 'workmen's cottages'. At the same time, surprisingly, Welwyn Rural District Council started building 50 houses, designed by de Soissons, in Elm Gardens and Applecroft Road. Although the Garden City had begun in the ecclesiastical parish and rural district of Hatfield, when its civil parish was created in 1921 it came under the aegis of Welwyn Rural District Council. Welwyn Garden City Urban District Council was created in 1927. This involved substantial changes in administrative

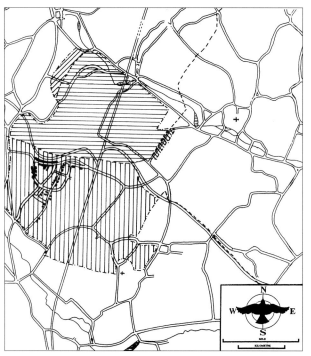

boundaries since it consisted of a large part of Hatfield north of the Lea, most of Digswell, a small part of Welwyn and a small portion of Hertford Rural District.

The choice of materials in the Garden City was limited to locally produced red brick, and cheap imported tiles. This lent itself to architecture in a style now called 'neo-Georgian' (George V!). One of the advantages of the Georgian style is that it makes use of a 'kit of parts' and a range of off-the-peg details. Among the smaller houses produced by the Company and its subsidiaries there were stand-ard patterns, which were given names and numbers. The overall impression is of 'theme and variations'.

104 Creation of the Rural District of Welwyn Garden City in 1927. Horizontal shading represents land annexed from Digswell; vertical shading land annexed from Hatfield; and diagonal shading land annexed from Welwyn in the west, and from Tewin (in Hertford Rural District) in the east.

105 Some of the 'concrete' houses being built. What would the Health and Safety Executive say today?

106 Lower Handside Farm was the New Towns Trust's hostel in the early days.

Public Utility Societies

Advantage was taken of government loans made available to 'public utility societies', the equivalent of modern housing associations, by the Housing Act of 1919, and several schemes were constructed in this way. One of them, Welwyn PUS, was inevitably a subsidiary of the Company. In 1924 the WPUS built 500 cheap terraced dwellings in a material that was similar to old-fashioned 'cob', a mixture of chalk and cement rammed into shuttering *in situ*. Unfortunately, unlike cob, the concrete was rigid; but the shallow foundations were on clay and there were no movement joints so the walls cracked. In addition they were not insulated and condensation formed on the insides. Ninety-three houses in Guessens Road, erected by the RDC without cavity walls or bathrooms, were demolished and replaced in the early 1970s. The 'concrete' houses in Broadwater Road and Ludwick Way were replaced by a much higher density development in the late 1970s, and those on Longcroft Lane at the end of the 1990s.

New Town Builders Ltd. was a subsidiary of the New Towns Trust. Its object was to produce communal settlements, and by May 1922 they had turned Lower Handside farmhouse into a hostel for young members of the Agricultural Guild. A co-operative scheme of flats with between one and three bedrooms was constructed, with common kitchen, dining, recreation rooms, laundry, garden and tennis courts, which became Guessens Court.

Company Weakness

In 1924 a series of six-per-cent development bond issues, redeemable in 1934 at 105 per cent, was begun. By 1925 and 1926 there was a net profit, but the directors had still not recommended payment of a dividend. In 1928 the fundamental weakness in the company's organisation became apparent. There was no managing director, and Purdom, the financial director, used his position to affect decision making at all levels. Seven principal officers, backed by Reiss, threatened to resign. The company's auditor, Sir Harry Peat, ineffectually attempted a reconciliation, and called for a stronger administration. Purdom

107   The Garden City's first bank.

resigned first as managing director of Welwyn Stores and Welwyn Restaurants and, shortly afterwards, as a director of the Company.

Reorganisation and Reconstruction

In 1929, after an investigation by the Ministry of Health instigated by the displaced Purdom, the finances of the Stores were reorganised. The subsidiary became Welwyn Stores (1929) Ltd. At the same time two chartered accountants joined the Board: F.M.Page as secretary and John Eccles as financial director. In 1931 a 'financial reconstruction' of the Company became necessary, and debenture bonds and debenture stock were converted to six per cent and seven per cent respectively. In 1931, during the depression, staff wages were cut and the directors agreed to 'a substantial reduction in their personal remuneration'.

The land at Stanborough Farm, which Howard had not been able to afford, became a thorn in the Company's side. Land south of Tinkers Hill, which was renamed Lemsford Lane, did not belong to Welwyn Garden City. A number of small businesses were set up in there in competition with the monopolies on the other side of the road. These included J.W.Sault's Welwyn Publications, Underwood hardware and Handside Nurseries. Underwood moved and the others were successively bought out by the Company. Most of the land was owned by a newly formed company, Stanborough Estates Ltd., of which Theodore Chambers somehow became chairman in 1928; two of its directors resigned and were replaced by Col. Freemantle and R.L. Reiss, both of whom were directors of the Company, and on 4 April

108   Air-raid shelters being dug on the Campus at the beginning of the Second World War.

1932 all its assets were transferred to Welwyn Garden City.

Another Reconstruction

In 1934 came another 'financial reconstruction'. Holders of debenture stock lost a total of £238,044. The bonds of the Public Utilities Society Ltd. and the income stock of the New Towns Trust were converted into Company shares, which, abandoning Howard's early principles, no longer placed an upper limit to the dividend. Ordinary £1 shareholders lost 18s. on each share.

When the Company had been first floated, a group of shareholders, mostly directors, had bought 93,500 unsold £1 shares at 1s. each. This seemed at the time to be a heroic gesture of confidence since, although they would benefit from the full dividend if the company succeeded, they also stood to lose £93,500 if it failed. It now emerged that they had sold 6,500 shares to the New Towns Trust, which had paid the full sum for them, and transferred the rest to a limited liability holding which could not pay for them. Of the total of £419,375 they lost only £435 and the New Towns Trust lost £5,850.

The Company began making administrative charges to its ramifying subsidiaries. The way in which the accounts were published was changed. In 1935, 'The profit and loss account discloses a profit of £112 compared with a deficit of £21,381 last year but, owing to the Scheme of Rearrangement, the two figures are not comparable.' The Company paid a dividend in 1936 of two per cent and dividend payments never exceeded six per cent.

At the beginning of the war, when building practically stopped, about 5,000 houses had been constructed and there were 5,143 households. The population had risen from 767 in 1921 to about 21,000, but this was suddenly boosted by an influx of 2,600 evacuees of whom 1,300 were schoolchildren.

Eight

Town Structure

The Layout

C.M. Crickmer, one of the architects of Letchworth, produced a layout plan which was rejected. With no master plan work began willy-nilly. Captain James was appointed chief civil engineer. Handside Lane, one of the few lanes that was better than a dirt track, was tarred, Crickmer designed 50 houses to be built there, and the old well at Handside was deepened to provide fresh water.

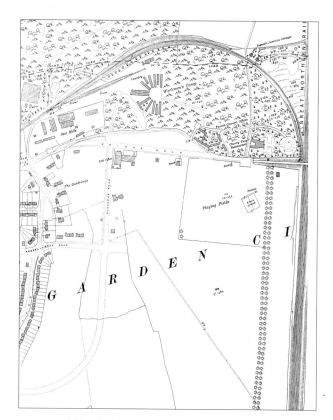

109 Ordnance Survey map of the town centre area in 1925.

A great deal has been written about the genius of the design of the Garden City. This is being wise after the event. When appointed, Louis de Soissons, although academically outstanding, was relatively inexperienced and was desperately short of money. He had before him valuable object lessons from Letchworth and Hampstead Garden Suburb.

The Company intended to provide the infrastructure of roads and services, but it was not anticipated that it should do all the building work. Indeed, capital was not available. Private companies and the local authority were encouraged to finance building, but some of the first houses, built by and for individuals in High Oaks Road, and by the *Daily Mail* at Meadow Green, failed to fit properly into the scheme. Through regulations the Company soon took a firm grip on materials and design (as on practically everything else), and de Soissons had 'almost complete control' of the work of other architects.

The construction gangs lived in ex-army huts where the Campus is today. Bricks were made beside the Luton branch line near the present Roundwood Drive and by the main line in what had been Lord Salisbury's pit (now Burrowfield), which also supplied sand and gravel, as did the pits at Digswell Water. A light narrow-gauge railway was used to transport building materials, agricultural produce, and even household furniture. It connected Horn's sidings, the gravel pits and brickworks and the model dairy with permanent ways, but it was a fairly simple matter to lay temporary track as necessary to construction sites.

The Master Plan

De Soissons produced a now-famous master plan designed to accommodate the existing road structure, the position of the main railway and the location of

110 Workmen's huts on the site of the Campus in about 1920.

111 A brick kiln in Sherrardspark Wood.

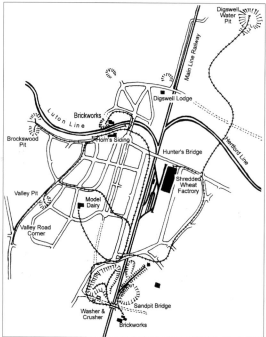

112 One of the Company's waggons being filled from the light railway at the sand and gravel works.

113 Light railways before the war. It was a relatively easy matter to provide temporary sidings to building sites.

the bridges, as well as the contours of the site. It is difficult today, now the city has materialised, to imagine any other, but the layout of the Garden City was fundamentally flawed by the broad swathe cut by the main line. The GNR insisted from the start, however, that no building should take place within an unbridgeable north-south swathe one-eighth of a mile (170m.) wide either side of their main line. The site slopes from west to east, and an east-west axis, which would have been ideal for the town centre, was adopted on Osborn's and Crickmer's initial plans. De Soisson's scheme had to employ a north-south axis, parallel to and west of the railway. Howard's concept of a central park became a broad avenue,

114   The light railway at Valley Road Corner in around 1930.

Parkway, on the west side. The town centre, administrative and commercial buildings were to be here, with a shorter avenue leading to the station. The industrial area had to be served by sidings and so, instead of being on the perimeter, as on Howard's diagram, it was sited on the east side of the main line. Despite its avowed egalitarian aims, the Company put the middle- and upper-class dwellings near the commercial and administrative centre on the west. The working-class housing was on the east, isolated by the railway and the industrial area, inevitably leading to a social divide and to people feeling they were 'on the wrong side of the tracks'. In vain the Company directors later argued that there were as many council tenants on the west as on the east, not mentioning the location of the houses in which they themselves lived.

The main line could be crossed only in three places on the Company's land: in the south, at Twentieth Mile Bridge by Stanborough Lane; in the middle, at Hunter's Bridge by an unmetalled track (a continuation of Brockswood Lane – later improved to become Bridge Road); and, a short

distance north of this, near Digswell Lodge Farm, on Lyle's Bridge by another track (now Digswell Rise). Lyle's Bridge was inaccessible because there were no vehicular crossings over the branch lines within the estate, and so Welwyn was reached via Brockswood Lane and the Great North Road. A bridgehead to the north was finally established when the White Bridge, designed by Louis de Soissons with elegant baroque 'pepper-pot' decoration, was opened in 1925. The Garden City then crossed the Hatfield parish boundary as well as the Luton branch railway line and effectively invaded Digswell. Lyle's Bridge provided access to the industrial area until it was closed to traffic after a new Knightsfield bridge was opened by the Development Corporation in November 1962.

The Lanes

To save money the Company did not construct new roads but mainly improved existing poorly-metalled ones, starting at Handside, which had both access to the Great North Road and a well capable of providing water for the project. The routes of

115 De Soissons' 1920 master plan for the Garden City. Although it is much praised, in practice only part of the south-west portion was actually realised.

116 The town centre from the south east in 1959, showing clearly its formal layout, the residential development in the background, the industrial area in the foreground, and the wide swathe cut by the railway.

these original tracks can still be traced as they are called 'Lanes' on the town map. New roads, culs-de-sac, closes and so on were constructed using gravel extracted on site. They were given names taken mainly from local place-names, especially from the 1837 Tithe Apportionment, and sometimes taken from quite distant places, by people who never anticipated that the town would eventually reach far enough to cause confusion. None of the new ways was called a 'street' as the word was redolent of smoky towns.

In the early years the roads were churned up by traffic, and the expression 'gum-boot era' was coined. It was suggested that the roads should be included in the company's 'liquid' assets, and a story current at that time told of someone discovering a bowler hat in the road, and on picking it up finding a man underneath! One subject of dispute between residents and the company in the early days was the proposal to put the responsibility for the roads in the hands of the Council. The residents pointed out that they had already paid in their leases for the infrastructure, and would now be asked to spend more in rates. There was no bus service in the town until 1923, when a bus ran to Hatfield and St Albans – on Tuesdays and Sundays!

Hunter's Bridge soon proved inadequate. The railway company refused to improve it and, despite

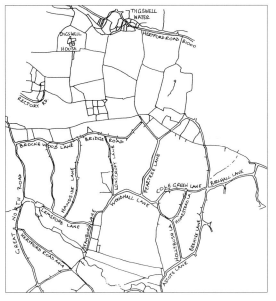

117 A map redrawn from the 1599 survey of Digswell and an undated early 16th-century map of Hatfield. The names of the modern Garden City 'lanes' have been added.

opposition from the Ministry of Transport who wanted to avoid a precedent being created, the Garden City Company were forced to widen it themselves in 1929-30. It was widened again and turned into a dual carriageway in 1960.

MUD MODES.
THE GUM BOOT SEASON IN OUR GARDEN CITY. A TRIUMPH OF SPARTAN ORGANISATION.

Shops

It is said that in the early days of the Garden City goods were sold from one of the temporary huts. At the outset, pragmatically contradicting his original ideals which required the Garden City to have a retail monopoly, and against the wishes of the other directors, Howard approached Selfridges and the St Albans Co-op about opening shops in the new town. They declined.

Welwyn [*sic*] Stores was founded in 1921, a subsidiary of the Company given a monopoly on the Company's land for ten years, a fact which did not go uncriticised. It opened in October in a building like a small 'blister hangar', at first selling food and then hardware. It became a general store. Its managing director was, of course, Purdom, who later wrote, 'Practically everything was wrong … the counters and fittings were not properly considered; the layout was faulty … there was no provision for a bakery or dairy …'. An attraction, however, was evening opening which enabled shoppers to listen to the Marconi House

118 This *Punch* cartoon illustrated the Gum Boot era.

119 The first Welwyn Stores, with Guessens Road in the background. The date is unknown but the empty shop windows suggest the picture was taken after the new store opened in 1939.

120   Aerial view of Welwyn Stores before the war.

concerts on a crystal set. In 1923 an extension, Parkway Hall, provided refreshments, and 'Kinema' shows on Tuesday and Saturday evenings, with Saturday matinées. A branch was opened at Peartree in 1925. In 1928, after Purdom had resigned and the financial structure been changed, the new public company, Welwyn Stores (1929) Ltd., with 90 per cent of its shares owned by the Garden City Company, was managed by Major Lemmens.

Competition

Despite their evident wish to maintain a virtual monopoly of trade, the Garden City Company did allocate premises to competing shops. Munts initially opened a cycle shop in 1927 in a hut over the Company's boundary at Tinkers Hill, but were invited to take over part of the builders' yard in Bridge Road and by 1928 had

newly-constructed premises in Stonehills, where they sold cycles, prams and toys. W.H. Smith opened one of the first shops on Howardsgate, at the corner of Wigmores South in July 1930, and they were joined in February 1931 by Donald Black, who sold children's wear. M. Berry opened a chemist's in April, when the Stores' covenanted monopoly ended. Underwood's hardware store, which had also begun at Tinkers Hill, moved to large premises in Howardsgate in 1934 after a short period next to the Welwyn Theatre in Parkway.

Post-War Shopping

After the war Welwyn Stores purchased shops outside the city including a grocer's in Hertford. It was a major asset to the Garden City Company, providing two-thirds of the Company's gross income of £1,560,000 by 1947.

121 Howardsgate from Stonehills in 1966. The shops have since had a top floor added, with a steel frame and 'geometric tile' cladding.

An Economic Survey

The early 1930s were years of economic depression. An independent economic survey produced at that time of the Company's 'financial restructuring' in 1934 indicated, not unexpectedly, that compared with the country as a whole Welwyn Garden City had a high proportion of children and a low one of elderly people. There was a high ratio of white-collar workers to manual ones, and a third of employees had an income over £250 per year, compared with a national ratio of one eighth. There was also a low proportion of domestic servants, either due to the design of labour-saving homes, the political views of the householders or lack of availability. Fifteen to twenty per cent of the working population commuted to London and there was a risk that, unless more working-class homes were provided, the town would become a dormitory.

The first part of a more permanent Welwyn Stores, housing fabrics and ladies' wear, had been opened on Parkway in October 1933 but, according to the report, the Stores were in trouble. Only the hardware and tobacco departments held their own. Food and perishable goods were making a substantial loss, and much trade was being lost to hawkers. An efficient delivery system would help, and would restore good will. The quarters were too small, and there should be fewer departments. The much-needed comprehensive buying and merchandising policy was 'beyond the scope of the acting management'. J.F. Eccles became managing director in 1934.

One recommendation may have surprised the Company: that more private traders were needed so that the town would be looked upon as a shopping centre. New shops were begun in Howardsgate in 1935. The St Albans Co-op opened on the corner of Wigmores South opposite Smith's in 1937. A new branch of Welwyn Stores was opened at Woodhall in October 1938.

122 Welwyn Stores in 1950.

The foundation stone of the Stores 'largest out-of-town department store' (now John Lewis) was laid by Chambers in July 1938. Designed by de Soissons, the shop opened in June 1939. It included 62 flats and, significantly, a Masonic Suite. Part of the original Stores became a council depot and was demolished in 1963 to make way for Rosanne House. When the war stopped further development, much of the town centre was still open space. Howardsgate had three banks, the Halifax Building Society and gas and electricity showrooms, as well as Cresta Silks, opticians, a tobacconist, hairdresser, confectioner, dry-cleaner and a music shop.

Perrings, house furnishers, were on the corner of Fretherne Road.

Garden City Industries

The provision of modern industry in the Garden City required the labour force, essential raw materials and energy sources to be brought into a rural area as concurrently as possible. Raw materials were not a problem; the site was served by the railway, even if this meant locating the industrial area across the centre of the site, exacerbating the potential east-west split dictated in part by the railway itself. The labour supply was another matter. The provision of essential services, 'infrastructure' and housing absorbed the attentions and the income of the early Company. Agriculture, despite being one of Howard's fundamental aims, would not support many so, at first, places to live 'in the country' were provided before places to work. The Garden City began as, and largely remained, a dormitory town.

Manufacturing industries needed to be attracted. In 1920 advertisements in the press and on hoardings for 'the Hertfordshire Highlands' stressed the low rates, services and clean atmosphere; the Company's logo misleadingly stressed the altitude. In an account of this size it is only possible to mention

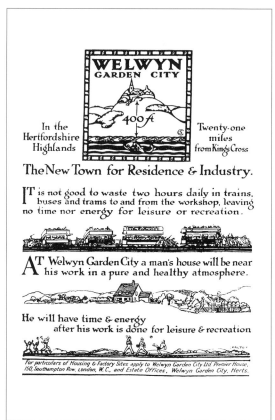

123 Early posters advertised the healthy environment. The pond at Meadow Green, into which outraged residents threw the Daily Mail Ideal Village advertisement, was later filled in as a health risk.

124 Misleading publicity? The only part of the Garden City above the 350ft contour at the time this poster was produced was the distant reservoir; there has never been a spire (and it isn't a city).

some of the firms which became associated with the Garden City, selecting arbitrarily on the grounds of size, contribution to the town or general interest. Collectors, for example, might wish to know that the Welwyn Match Manufacturing Co. and the Southern Match Co. operated in Broadwater Road from 1932-4.

The First Factories

Apart from subsidiaries of the Company, the first factory, started in 1923 on the north-east side of Hunter's Bridge, was a steel depot for Dorman Long, soon taken over by Dawnay & Sons who

eventually occupied five acres and employed a workforce of 150 and more. The company became a subsidiary of British Steel and the factory was closed in 1969. There was also a foundry in Bessemer Road from 1927 which made, among other things, gutters, drainpipes and Ideal Boilers, which were used in many local houses.

The healthy image of the town attracted the American firm, Shredded Wheat Company, and their factory ('a palace of crystal') started production in 1925 with 100 workers. The product was 'Welgar' (from WELwyn GARden) Shredded Wheat. Taken over by National Biscuit Company

125   The interior of Dawnay's steel works before the Second World War.

126   Welgar Shredded Wheat factory decorated for the visit of King George VI in 1939.

127 Repairing subsidence in Broadwater Road in 1973. The original sectional buildings are in the background.

(Nabisco) in 1928, it has a staff of about 1,000 and manufactures a wide range of farinaceous products; tall silos store wheat, of which it uses about 400 tons per week.

By 1926 Welwyn Garden City Ltd. had begun to build what are today called 'units' – small single-storeyed buildings divided into sections which the tenants could sub-divide with their own partitions. These attracted small businesses with limited capital, particularly innovative 'modern' ones, such as those making domestic electrical equipment. Among the applicants was Frank Murphy, who wanted a 'workshop where radio experiments could be carried out'. The BBC had begun broadcasting in 1922 and 'radio sets' using valves were replacing 'crystal sets' with 'cats' whiskers'. In 1928 Murphy moved from a garage in Brockswood Lane to a unit in Broadwater Road, and by the end of the year had a workforce of seventy. In 1933 the company built and enlarged its own factory and there were over 500 employees. By the beginning of the war it was one of the world's six largest electronic firms. After performing important war work, and with the advent of television, a modern factory with 329,400 square feet of floorspace was

128 The impressive Murphy Radio factory in 1955.

129 Welwyn Film Studios from the north-west in 1928. The land in the foreground belonged to the railway. Peartree is in the background – on the 'wrong side of the tracks'.

progressively built between 1954 and 1959 on a site between Bessemer Road and the railway. The hard-pressed Development Corporation were relieved; Murphy's finally vacated a large number of units, making them available for others to use. At the same time Aviation Development (Avdel), moved into their new works, releasing a further 23,600 square feet of units. Murphy became Rank Bush Murphy in 1962, and in 1970 the electronics division moved to Ware. The factory, fifty years ago one of the Corporation's show pieces, has been demolished.

British Instructional Films Studio was built by Dawnays between Broadwater Road and the railway in 1928. Seventy-two films were made in the first three years. In 1935 Pathe started filming there. The studios were closed by Associated Pictures Corporation in 1952, and Ardath Tobacco made cigarettes there until 1960. In 1962 the studios became the nucleus of the works of Polycel.

Outgrowing its Strength

By the 1930s, against all the odds, there was a shortage of labour in the town and families were being imported from South Wales and Clydeside under a Ministry Industrial Transfer Scheme.

In 1929 an exhibition of Welwyn industries had attracted 35 companies, the Chamber of Commerce was started, and a labour exchange opened. Norton Grinding Wheel Ltd. was the next major firm to arrive. Its purpose-built factory beside the Hertford line, occupied in 1931, was the largest in the town and employed over 1,000 workers. As Norton Abrasives it built a £1,000,000 office block in Bridge Road East in 1963. Work was transferred to other plants abroad in 1982.

In 1933 a subsidiary of ICI, which made synthetic resins and moulding powders, Croydon Moldright Co. arrived. Eventually ICI itself occupied a ten-acre site housing the plant and headquarters of its Plastics Division, which became the largest plastics manufacturer in the Commonwealth. During the war it used The Hall, Welwyn as a research laboratory, Lockleys and Guessens as hostels, and later The Frythe for research. Production went to the north of England in the 1950s, but sales, technical services, research and development stayed. Closed in 1985, the works were demolished and the site is now Shire Park.

Lincoln Electric, specialising in welding equipment, arrived in Broadwater Road in 1935, and expanded in 1937 and 1949, moving into a 180,000 sq. ft. factory beside the Hertford line in 1957. In

130   The ICI site, now Shire Park, in 1976. Mundells is in the foreground.

131   Lincoln Electric's factory seen from the west in 1960. It lay at the end of Black Fan Road before the latter was extended to Birchall Lane. Attimore Farm is seen across Ridgeway and the level crossing is on the right of the picture.

1952 it had become a subsidiary of GKN, which was itself taken over by Esab in 1982. The plant moved to Stevenage and the factory was demolished. The site is now mainly warehouses.

Hoffman la Roche, the pharmaceuticals firm, transferred their UK operation and 240 employees to a site beside the Film Studio in 1938. Roche Products nowadays employs about 1,000 people in a modern factory built in 1973 in Broadwater Road, and is best known for Librium and Valium. Close to Roche is Polypenco, who make nylon rod and industrial castings.

In 1959 Smith Kline and French Ltd. began what was to become the town's tallest building at

132   The Barcley Corsets factory. Listed for its outstanding design, it was demolished in 2000 to make way for a Rover Cars dealer.

Mundells. They have a ten-acre farm in Ridgeway and took over The Frythe laboratories from Unilever. As a result of a series of take-overs and mergers, the company is now part of one of the largest drug producers, GlaxoSmithKline.

Vincenti Lunardi in 1784 passed over the area in the first man-carrying balloon without landing. The local aviation tradition was extended by the many inhabitants employed at the aircraft works at Hatfield started by De Havilland in 1928. Before the Second World War De Havilland's also bought and cleared 180 acres of well-drained flat arable land to the east for use as an apprentice school and all-grass landing ground. It was called, at first, Holwell Hyde aerodrome, and later Panshanger airfield. At the beginning of the war it became a dummy airfield with mock aircraft and stocks of fuel ready to create 'conflagrations', the object being to confuse an enemy attack and divert it away from

Hatfield. Later it reverted to its earlier role, part being used during the development of the DH Mosquito and part by the RAF as No.1 Elementary Flying School, using Tiger Moths. The London Flying Club took over the north of the site after the war, while the RAFVR continued to fly Chipmunks until 1953, when the Development Corporation bought their land, which has since been progressively built upon, reducing the airfield area to its present 100 acres. The Panshanger School of Flying was there from 1982-92, and the site is still used as a flying school.

Education

Welwyn Garden City Ltd. had given little thought to education. One of the terms of the agreement negotiated by the Pioneer Trust was that an Educational Association should be set up. It was formally constituted as a trust in 1922 and owned

133   The High School, Digswell Road. Founded in 1927 for boys and girls aged five to 18, it became Sherrardswood School in 1942.

Lawrence Hall, Trevelyan House and the Backhouse Room, as well as providing schools with libraries. There were nine directors, two each from the Urban District Council and the Company, plus two managers and another from the WGC Health Association.

The first meeting of school managers (most of whom were directors of the Association) was in October of that year, and Handside co-educational modern school for 400 pupils (later renamed Applecroft) was begun by the County Council. The High School, which was renamed Sherrardswood School in 1942, was an independent foundation in 1928. Its original premises, between the White Bridge and Sherrardspark Road, have now become a housing estate; boarders at the school made use of Digswell House, as well as Guessens and Lockleys in Welwyn. It is now a junior and senior day school in Lockleys, which it acquired in 1955. Ludwick infants school and Parkway junior school, where its pupils transferred

at seven years of age, opened in 1932 and 1934 respectively, and the Grammar School in 1939, just in time to be almost swamped by evacuees from London.

During the inter-war period there were a number of private and other schools in the town. According to the year-book for 1929, Fretherne House preparatory school for boys (1926) and Claddagh School for girls (1927) were in the building which later became the Cottage Hospital and is now a restaurant. The Alpha School was for boys aged from five to 10 and girls from five to 18 years. In 1931 the Canossian RC Convent was for girls over four years old, and Snelsmore School was in the Backhouse Room in 1932. In 1935 the Montessori Children's House was purpose built in Handside Close, and there was also Peartree Junior County, Snelsmore House for girls aged three to 10 and boys aged three to eight in the Friends Meeting House, and the School of Music in Elmwood. Croft

134   Heronswood School in 1958.

kindergarten and preparatory school appears in 1936, and dancing, secretarial, and nursery schools in 1937.

After the war the 1944 Education Act, coupled with the rapid expansion of the New Town, led to the creation of a large number of schools. The Howard Secondary Modern School opened in 1953 and Attimore Secondary Modern School and High Schools opened on adjoining sites in Herns Lane in 1956 and 1960. Heronswood Secondary Modern opened in 1956. The Mater Dei RC school for girls aged four to 18 and boys aged four to nine opened in 1962; St Joseph's Roman Catholic Secondary School for boys opened in 1967.

The change to comprehensive education led to the Grammar School being renamed Stanborough School in 1968. A secondary modern and a grammar school which were under construction on the same site in the north-west were combined to form Monks Walk comprehensive school, which opened in 1964, and the High School and Attimore School combined as a comprehensive named after Frederic Osborn.

Despite the raising of the school-leaving age in 1972 the school population began to fall. St Joseph's merged with the Mater Dei, which was renamed Holy Trinity in 1981 but it closed in 1986. The

Mater Dei convent was developed for housing. In 1987 Heronswood merged with the Howard School, becoming the Sir John Newsome School, and Heronswood has become a housing estate. Sir John Newsome has since merged with the Stanborough School on the latter's site, because the younger and better-equipped school, unlike Stanborough, was not in the green belt and could be sold for development.

Further education was served by the Mid Herts College which was opened on the Campus by

135   The Grammar School in 1968.

136   Peartree Farm was a maternity hospital in the early 1960s.

HRH Princess Alexandra of Kent on 19 November 1960. The building incorporated a new county library. As a result of amalgamations, it was renamed De Havilland College in 1979 and became part of Oaklands College in 1991.

A large number of post-war primary and nursery schools, often of outstandingly good design, were erected by the County Council. They too have suffered mergers and redevelopment. There are currently 22 such schools in our area.

Hospitals

In 1922 Danesbury House was sold by Michael Dewar to Middlesex County Council and used for convalescents and, later, by incurably ill patients until another hospital, 'New Danesbury', was opened beside the Queen Victoria Hospital in 1994.

A larger, 30-bed Queen Victoria Hospital in School Lane, made possible by a £25,000 donation from Sir Otto Beit of Tewin Water, replaced the Codicote Road one in 1934. Other donations came from Lord Lytton (Knebworth), Col. Acland (Digswell House) and Lord and Lady Brocket; the land was given by the Wilsheres of The Frythe. Patients were being admitted from a wider area, including the Ayots, Tewin and Wheathampstead. One fifth of nearly one thousand admissions were from the Garden City. Fund-raising events have been organised to support the hospital, to buy equipment and to build extensions ever since.

Despite the Garden City Company's propaganda, it seems that no initial provision was made for health care. The nearest doctors paid calls from Hatfield and Welwyn but most of the roads were muddy tracks and the White Bridge did not exist. The nearest chemist was in Hatfield. In January 1921 Lord Dawson, the King's Physician, was invited by residents to talk on health resources and a committee was formed to set up a scheme. In March 1922 Dr. Fry and his wife Dr. Miall-Smith (who had been dismissed from her post in London because she married) became residents at the invitation of Reiss, a school friend of Dr. Fry. A Health Council met in April, and formed first-aid and infant welfare committees. The barber's hut on the Campus became the first aid post and the Company agreed to contribute towards it a penny a week per employee.

An infant welfare clinic was held from May in the Meeting Room which was provided free by the Company. Dr. Miall-Smith and Mrs. Smart, a trained health visitor, gave their services and a rota of volunteers was organised. Subscriptions of a penny a week were collected. There was a district nurse and charges were made for visits. Dr. Furnival arrived in July. He built Russells, where he lived with his wife and five children, and other doctors followed.

In June 1923 there were 62 attendances at the clinic. Dr. Miall-Smith was appointed salaried medical officer to the clinic for which purpose a grant was obtained from the Ministry of Health. Welwyn Stores appointed a pharmacist. A private nursing home, The Hollies, was created from two houses at the corner of Youngs Rise and Elm Gardens. It took charge of the first-aid equipment, and the welfare clinic moved into the Lawrence Hall. A dental service was provided and the New Towns Trust offered the use of a laundry car as an ambulance.

The Health Association

The informal organisation became the Health Association in 1925 and The Hollies allocated it two beds. In 1927 there were stretchers at the fire station and an arrangement with Hertford Hospital for use of an ambulance at half cost, and a community trust was set up by local employers to help both Health and Educational Associations. Home helps were provided. In addition a Guild of Health, representing a wide range of bodies, provided all kinds of assistance; it was wound up when the National Health Service was started in 1948. A separate child welfare clinic was started at Peartree clubhouse, and in 1928 Dr. Fry started the local St John's Ambulance Brigade, keeping an ambulance behind the Stores.

In January 1929 The Hollies was bought and became the Cottage Hospital; by increasing their subscription, Association members could have beds

137 The Queen Elizabeth II Hospital just before the official opening in July 1963.

at a reduced rate. There were eight beds; three were private. An operating theatre was created for general surgery, although specialists were available. In six months there were 62 admissions, and fundraising schemes for an even larger hospital were considered.

In 1940 the Garden City's Cottage Hospital moved into Fretherne House, which had been vacated by the Rev. Whalley's school. Funds were still raised by subscription and charitable events until 1948. Peartree Boys' Club had been provided in 1937 with dormitory accommodation for young men from depressed areas who found work in the Garden City, and use was made of these dormitories as a maternity hospital for evacuees. They continued to be used by the county in this way until the new hospital opened in 1963. Brocket Hall was also used as a maternity hospital during the Second World War, and 4,313 boys and 4,025 girls were born there in this period.

In 1954 the Development Corporation began discussions with the North West Metropolitan Board for a large hospital for the New Town. The present 330-bed hospital was begun on 22 acres close to the Salisbury Line at The Commons in March 1958. It was officially opened by Her Majesty Queen Elizabeth II and named after her in July 1963. The maternity hospital in Peartree Lane became a YMCA hostel.

Religions

Church of England services were provided by the Hatfield curate for the first inhabitants of the Garden

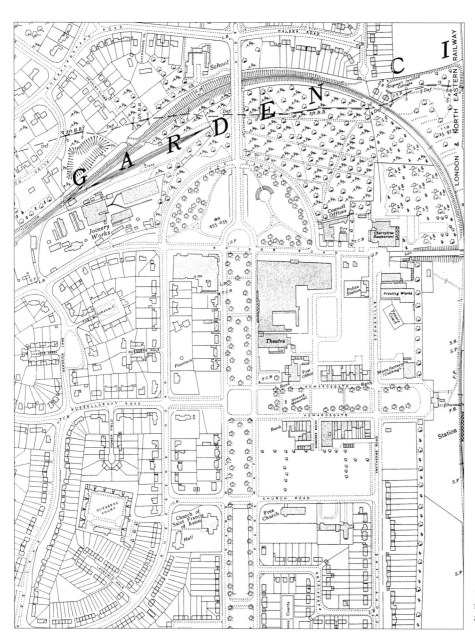

138 Ordnance Survey map of the town centre area in 1939.

City in one of the wooden huts on Bridge Road at the Campus site, evensong being celebrated every Sunday from May 1921, and Holy Communion on Wednesdays. St Francis' church hall was dedicated in 1923, and was shared by other denominations. The parish was created in 1927. The church was consecrated in 1935, but was not completed to the original ambitious design. The present hall and ancillary rooms date from 1976. The original hall has been demolished. A striking small chapel was built beside Tewin Road by Donald Carnegie of Carnegie Chemicals. It ceased to be used as a chapel when the firm changed hands and was converted into an office.

There were citizens of many religious persuasions, and the annual directories show how they met in one another's homes and the various public halls, often sharing, sometimes exchanging. By 1935 there were Anglican services at Church Road (St Francis'), Ludwick Way (St Michael's Hall), Digswell (St John's) and Hatfield Hyde (St Mary Magdalene), and services at the Free Church in Parkway (opened in 1929) and Hatfield Hyde. Roman Catholic masses were celebrated at the Convent in Parkway, and St Bonaventure's opened in 1926. The Friends Meeting House was built in 1926 at Lower Handside Farm; they had met previously in the Backhouse Room (Lower Handside Farm). The Congregationalists met in Hatfield Hyde Club Room; their church in Woodhall Lane was dedicated in 1928.

The Baptists were at Lawrence Hall in Applecroft Road; they had also met in the Children's House, next to Handside (Applecroft) School, at Alpha School, on the corner of Applecroft Road and Elmwood, and at the Backhouse Room, and they moved into their new place of worship, Christ Church, Parkway in 1940. Christian Scientists were at the High School, Christian Spiritualists at the School of Music (previously Alpha School) and Welwyn Garden City Full Gospel Mission Interdenominational in Longcroft Green.

Before the war the war the socially aware citizens concerned themselves with the plight of the Jews in Nazi Germany. Richard Reiss gave a house for the use of refugees, and there is a garden on Parkway: 'Established with gratitude to Capt R.L. Reiss, Edgar Reissner and the citizens of Welwyn Garden City by the fourteen young Jewish men rescued by Wim Van Leer from German concentration camps after the "Kristall Nacht" in November 1938.' The Jewish community met in the Friends Meeting House until the Synagogue was built in Handside Lane in 1956.

The long history of unsympathetic treatment of Digswell church culminated in 1960 in total demolition of the south wall and porch without any proper record of it being made, the levelling of the churchyard on this side, and the attachment of a modern, barn-like extension. In 1961 the RC Church of Our Lady Queen of the Apostles was opened in Woodhall Lane; a family centre was added to it in 1972. In Haldens the Church of Christ the King was consecrated in 1964. The Church of the

139   Friendship House, Tewin Road.

Holy Family was opened at Shoplands in 1967. An ecumenical Pastoral Care Centre was opened in Panshanger in 1977.

Pubs

West of the site of the proposed Garden City were *The Sun* and the *Long Arm and Short Arm* at Lemsford, and the *Red Lion* and *The Waggoners* on the Great North Road, the last two reached by a pleasant stroll through Sherrardspark Wood. Purdom wrote of *The Waggoners*: 'It was a mud-and-plaster erection standing on what had been roadside waste, with a strip of land at the back which had seemingly been stolen from the adjacent field. When the owner decided to sell … at the auction I raised the question of the land, and declared that the auctioneer had no title to sell according to his particulars, and … the place was knocked down to

140   The *Green Man*, Mill Green, around 1930.

141   The original *Cherry Tree* public house.

142   Welwyn Garden City swimming pool before the war.

us for £3,120 ... The figure was absurd.' Further away (and 'on the wrong side of the tracks') were the *Beehive*, bought by the Company in the 1919 auction, the *Woodman* at Hatfield Hyde and the *Green Man* at Mill Green.

Unlike Letchworth, Welwyn Garden was not to be teetotal. The Company understood the need for 'a wet canteen', particularly for the construction workers, and the outcome was the *Cherry Tree*, a wooden building described at the time as 'primitive and pioneer'. It was run by Welwyn Restaurants Ltd., a subsidiary of the Company. Further wooden huts were added to it and used by clubs and societies and it came to provide banqueting facilities.

By 1932 it was time to modernise and the task was put out to tender. Whitbread, although not the highest bidder, was appointed because 'its approach to management best fitted the ideals' of the Company. The assets were transferred to yet another organisation, 'The Improved Public House Company', with representatives of the Welwyn Garden City Company on the Board. The new company had the option to build new public houses, including a 'community centre pub'. R.G. Muir was the architect, and the new building was

completed by the beginning of 1933. The *Cherry Tree* became a Waitrose supermarket in 1991; its bowling green is now a car park.

In 1936 it was intended to build the *Pear Tree* beside the Company's store in Peartree Lane, but public opinion was against this. An alternative site at the junction of Mill Green Lane and Woodhall Lane was refused a licence until 1938. The *Woodman*, which was built in 1949, was extensively altered and renamed the *Chieftain* in 1978.

The neighbourhood centres of the New Town Plan required licensed premises: the *Hollybush* opened in 1958, the *Hedgehog* in 1962, the *Mayflower* (the first real 'community centre pub') in 1964, the *Fountain* in 1967 and the *Oak Tavern* in 1979. *The Cottage*, a licensed carvery, was opened in 1982; it had been Fretherne School, and then the Cottage Hospital, and is now the *Doctor's Tonic*. Recently licences have been granted to *Attimore Hall* and the *Fairway Tavern*.

Sport
Welwyn Garden City Football Club was founded in the early 1920s, and the Panshanger Club in the 1960s. The Rugby Club and the Ladies' Hockey Club were founded in about 1925. The first public

143   The Clock swimming pool, Welwyn before the war.

sports fields in the Garden City were at Handside, with pitches for rugby, association football, cricket and hockey. There was a bowls green beside the *Cherry Tree* which moved to Digswell Cricket Ground when Waitrose took over the site in 1991. King George V Playing Fields was acquired at Hatfield Hyde in 1932. At the outbreak of the war it was 'not yet fully laid out' but had four pitches for cricket, five for football and one for hockey. Since the war several additional recreational spaces have been added.

In the 1920s there was an open-air swimming pool at Mill Green, and until the outbreak of war in 1939 there was another at *The Clock*, Welwyn. The Garden City folk discussed use of a pit in Brockswood, the moat at Peartree and a site at the junction of Digswell Road and Bridge Road as possible swimming pools. When the Stanborough Estate was taken over, a site close to the Lea became available, and a Spartan pool was opened in June 1935. It was enlarged in 1960, and improvements were made to the building in 1964.

In 1999 the bottom fell out and it is said that a swallow hole makes re-opening unlikely.

When the gravel pits between Stanborough Lane and the railway were worked out, they were used as a dump for spoil from construction work and, during the war, by the army to train bull-dozer drivers. The idea of landscaping the site as a sports stadium was put forward, a project not within the remit of the Development Corporation. In 1958 an appeal in memory of R. Gosling, the Corporation's first chairman, was supported by the Urban District Council and industry, and the Gosling Stadium, with central green, cycling and running tracks was opened in July 1959. A club house was added in 1962. The site was taken over by an association which became a charitable trust in 1970, and they improved it over the years, with the addition of a golf range, dry ski slope and squash courts. The indoor sports complex which opened in 1976 cost £600,000, almost half of which was contributed by the District Council.

144 View over the new Chequers from the south in 1959. The old brick yard and sand pit, now the Burrowfield industrial estate, is in the centre. The Gosling Stadium, in another pit, is on its left.

Recreational Amenities

The Garden City's original concept does not seem to have provided for cultural amenities and its record on them contrasts greatly with that for more physical pursuits. It is typical that, when Howard died in 1928, a suggestion for a suitable memorial was a theatre or art gallery, but after four years a tiny brick wall with his name on it was built in Howardsgate, standing on a low mound, beneath which children believed Howard was interred! The wall was later accused of spoiling the vista and was replaced in 1964 by a tasteful bronze plaque which, being horizontal, is all but invisible. An art gallery, concert hall and museum were suggested as a war memorial in 1944, but in the event a small curved stone wall was erected – 35 years later!

Somebody once said that in the Garden City everybody was a member of several clubs and secretary of at least one. Many youth clubs and societies were formed, including a Boy Scout troop in the mid-1920s, Girl Guides in 1926 and a Boys' Brigade in 1927. Peartree club house was built in 1935, and the Boys' Club was founded the next year.

The problem at first was where to hold meetings. In 1920 one of the huts on the Campus was 'The Meeting Room'. The *Cherry Tree* provided another venue. In 1922 a cart shed at Upper Handside Farm was turned into a hall in memory of Edward Backhouse, a leading Quaker and member of the New Towns Trust, and the Lawrence Hall in Applecroft Road was built through the generosity of Mrs. Lawrence, with a grant of £800 from the

145 An early photograph of the Lawrence Hall.

146 Electric milking at Lower Handside in the 1920s. This is now the home of the Barn Theatre.

Educational Association conditional upon the hall's being used as an educational establishment and provided with craft training facilities.

There was always a great interest in amateur dramatics and in 1931 a cowshed at Lower Handside Farm was converted, with old cinema seating, into the Barn Theatre. The groups using it combined as Welwyn Drama Club and took it over, the only theatre in the county owned and run by amateurs. During the war the Barn was used by the army, and later by the Sea Training Corps. In 1969 the Drama Club and the Welwyn Folk Players formed a Barn Theatre Club, and in 1984 the club bought the theatre outright.

Moving pictures were shown in the public hall in London Road, Hatfield from 1913 to 1925, when the performances were moved to the Picture House. The Regent, opened in 1935 in Common Lane, became successively the Odeon, the Classic, the Curzon and the Chequers before it closed in 1969. The first film shows in the Garden City were in the Stores annex, but in 1928 Welwyn Theatre was opened in Parkway, with seating for about 1,200, and with a cinema monopoly on Company land. An amateur repertory company formed to use it failed and, although it was used for the Welwyn Drama Festival until Campus West was established, it was never a theatre. It was refurbished following a fire in 1963, renamed the Embassy Cinema in 1965, closed in 1983, and demolished. The Pavilion Cinema was built at the top of Welwyn Hill in 1935. It closed in 1963 and is now Godfrey Davis' garage.

In 1884 a social club and reading room, which later housed a branch of the county library, had been built at the corner of Ayot Green, between the *Red Lion* and *The Waggoners*. It was demolished when the motorway was built. In 1922 a book club run by volunteers was established in the Stores with donated books. Membership was 3s. and there was a free library in 1925. A branch of the county library was opened in the Lawrence Hall in 1926. The two libraries merged and grew, and the collection moved several times: to Upper Handside Farmhouse, the Company's old offices on the Campus and, by 1939, to Guessens Road. A mobile

147 The Embassy Cinema and Theatre in May 1981.

148 The Pavilion Cinema, Welwyn. This is now the entrance to Godfrey Davis.

library service started in 1959, and in 1960 the library moved into the new College building on Campus East. It moved to Campus West in 1973. There is a main library in Hatfield New Town, and a branch library at Woodhall.

Lemsford's original parish hall was opened in 1885 beside Bridge House but moved to Roebuck Farm and then to a field opposite. It is now dilapidated, and a new hall has recently been built by the church. Digswell's parish room of 1890 became the village hall. The present hall, near Welwyn North Station, dates from 1923 and was enlarged in the 1960s.

Nine

After the War

At the end of the war the Company foresaw rich pickings from the expected housing boom, and the proposed population was raised from 30,000 to 50,000. Howard's original ideals were finally abandoned. The notion of the majority of people working and living in the town had proved unattainable from the outset and an egalitarian mix of development had been forgotten so that the west side could be developed as middle-class. The seven per cent limit on dividends had been abandoned in 1934, and had never been applied to the Company's subsidiaries. More land was needed for more houses because the average number of people per household was falling.

In 1945 the Urban District Council erected 50 Phoenix prefabricated houses in Springfields and Marsden Road and began work on 212 houses and 16 flats in Hollybush Lane. The Company started work on 54 houses using money which it had borrowed, the Council standing surety for the loan, but instead of going ahead with the pre-war plan it bought more property on the north of the Mimram: Danesbury (202 acres) and Tewin Water (462 acres). It had already bought land outside the original remit in 1936: Lockleys, comprising 700 acres, including a considerable portion of Welwyn village.

There were protests, naturally, from Welwyn village, which was threatened with absorption. More land was purchased which did fit in with the original concept: 202 acres from the Panshanger Estate and 565 acres from Lord Salisbury. To ensure a 'green belt' between the Garden City and Hatfield, it was agreed that a strip of land, 'the Salisbury Line' between the Company's land and the Gascoyne-Cecil (Salisbury) estate, would remain undeveloped.

Before the war there had been vociferous objection to plans for building 'high-class' homes in Sherrardspark Wood, and the 'Save the Woods'

149 Demolition of Springfields' Phoenix 'pre-fabs', which had been built in 1945.

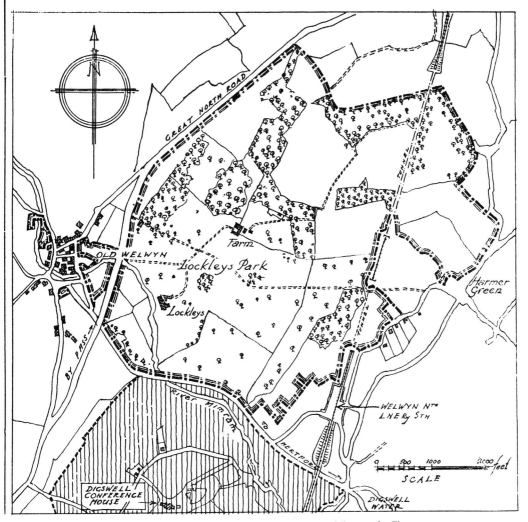

THE WELWYN TIMES

THURSDAY, OCTOBER 29, 1936

THE 700 ACRE ADDITION TO THE GARDEN CITY

The main Lockleys Estate is shown with a heavy dotted line round . The North Road forms the Western Boundary and on the North the boundary extends to Oaklands. On the South the boundary is the Hertford Road, which for about half a mile runs between the old and the new estates. The irregular Eastern boundary at one point crosses the main L.N.E.R. and extends to Harmer Green. In addition there are a number of separate smaller pieces of land in Old Welwyn, including "Guessens," "Parkside," the White Hart Inn and the Police Station.

150   The *Welwyn Times* announces the purchase of Lockleys by the Company in 1936.

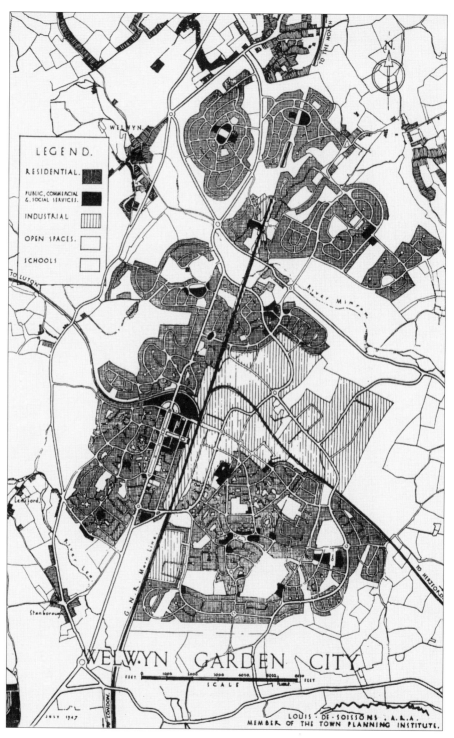

151 The layout proposed by the Company in 1947. It included Lockleys, Harmergreen
Wood, Welwyn North and most of the farmland between Harmer Green Lane and
Tewin (excluding the steep Dawley Wood).

Committee had been formed. It was revived in 1945, when the Council told the citizens that the Company was 'generous and public spirited' in allowing 64 per cent of the wood to remain as open space. To purchase the rest would have 'cost the ratepayers £75,000, which would best be spent on amenities for the Peartree area'. Many residents were more disturbed by what they saw as the 'secretive hand-in-glove association of the District Council and the Company'. The two shared officers, and directors of the Company were also elected members of the Council.

The *Welwyn Garden City Directory* was published annually by Welwyn Publications Ltd., another subsidiary of the Company. The 1947 edition makes the position the Company intended to maintain embarrassingly clear:

> The division of powers and responsibilities as between the Urban Council and the Welwyn Garden City Company is seldom grasped by outsiders and not always understood by people who live here. Briefly the position is this. The Urban Council, a democratically elected body, has exactly the same duties and obligations as any Urban Council elsewhere. The Company has exactly the same legal powers and responsibilities as any landowner elsewhere. The great difference consists in the fact that the Company is the sole landowner …

> In practice the Company puts forward various schemes for development, but all of these must be approved by the Council as the statutory Planning Authority for the whole Urban District. The absence of any serious dissension on these matters between the two authorities is due to a combination of facts. One of these is that, in Mr Louis de Soissons, the town possesses a planner whose prestige and experience in this type of work is unrivalled. The Council for its part has taken the line that it is its duty to scrutinize all planning proposals from the point of view of the public interest, examining each proposed piece of development on its merits. At the joint meetings which are held regularly both sides put their cards on the table and, as fundamentally their interests are identical – that is to enhance the prosperity and attractiveness of the town as a whole – their dissensions have been amicably solved.

At this time the Council was Labour dominated, and six Labour MPs were living in the town. Several councillors suggested that the Council should compulsorily purchase the Company's land. The 1944 Abercrombie 'Greater London Plan' had called for the creation of satellite towns, and representatives of the Council secretly approached the Minister of Town and Country Planning for the new Labour government, Lewis Silkin, in September 1946 and asked him to take the development of the town out of the hands of the Company. In February 1947 Silkin limited the town's growth to 36,500 and forbade expansion north of the Mimram. In June the Company offered to transfer the freehold of the town, when completed, to the local authority at an independent valuation, and in July provocatively published their proposed master plan which still included the land north of the Mimram. In mid-August Silkin replied that he would establish a Development Corporation for Welwyn [*sic*] and Hatfield under the New Towns Act of 1946. His primary objection – that the Company was not a democratically elected body – was illogical since the Corporation was an unelected quango. The Welwyn Garden City and Hatfield Development Corporations were established in June 1948 as two separate entities run by the same people from the same office.

New Town

Having resigned his interest in the Company and its subsidiaries, Richard Reiss became vice-chairman of the Garden City Corporation. Louis de Soissons remained in place as town planner and produced a new master plan. The Company's landscape architect, Malcolm Sefton, transferred to the Corporation, along with J. Skinner, the Company's engineer. H.T. Tigwell, who had served in the Company's financial department became comptroller. In general terms, therefore there was continuity.

Development was begun in the area of Woodland Rise and Reddings, where free rein was given to independent modern architects. Some disquiet was expressed at the results. In 1949 the Development Corporation submitted the new de Soissons master plan, which anticipated about the same density of population as Howard's original, but over a larger area. Four neighbourhood shopping centres were proposed, with health centres, churches, schools and nurseries conveniently placed nearby.

152   By 1959 Hatfield Hyde boasted shops, the *Hollybush* public house and a laundrette.

The Corporation was responsible for constructing these centres at Ludwick (1955), Handside (Hall Grove) and Woodhall (1954), and Hatfield Hyde (Hollybush) (1959). In 1959 temporary shops were opened in houses at Ingles; the shops were completed at Shoplands in the following year, and at Haldens in 1965.

The 1949 master plan reflects the proposed 36,500 population. However, by 1955 a population of 50,500 was planned, using land at what had come to be called Panshanger, the present north-eastern area of the town. Cheaper methods of building and standardised components were insisted upon. The result was that later development lacked the character which had been expected of the original Garden City. With the removal of the Company monopolies, the town centre was developed with shops and supermarkets.

In 1960, after 12 years under the Development Corporation, 4,400 new dwellings had been built and the population had risen by 11,000. There were 10 new schools, 42 new shops and over a million extra square feet of factory space.

Vanishing Assets

What happened to the assets of the Company and its subsidiaries is poorly documented and largely unpublished. In February 1950, we are told, 1s. 3d. per share was paid as compensation to the directors, amounting to £33,519. Initially, each Welwyn Garden City shareholder received 23s. 6d. in cash and 37s. 3d. worth of shares in a subsidiary of the Company, Howardsgate Trust, which is something of a puzzle.

In December 1939 'Howardsgate Investment Trust' had been established, with the Company

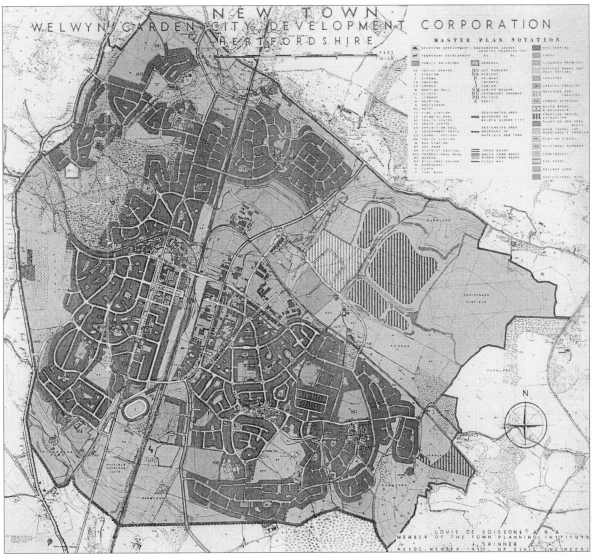

153   Welwyn Development Corporation's Master Plan of 1949.

holding 493 shares, and seven more being held by Chambers, Leonard Gray, and Reiss. In March 1948, however, at the public enquiry into the proposed takeover by the Development Corporation, Eccles stated that 'Howardsgate Trust Limited came into existence at the time of the recent reconstruction for the holding of shares which the Judge at the time had no other means of dealing with' and no financial reconstruction after 1934 is mentioned in the surviving archive. It seems likely that the two trusts were synonymous.

Howardsgate Trust took charge of the distribution to ordinary shareholders of the money remaining from the £2.8 million paid by the government after repayment of overdrafts, mortgages and redemption of preference shares. It also administered the Stores, Welwyn Builders, Welwyn Transport, Welwyn Electrical Installations, Cresta Silks, South-Eastern Bakeries and Digswell Nurseries. It set aside 'in trust' 38,107 ordinary shares in Welwyn Garden City Ltd. 'to charge, sell or mortgage', the income to be applied 'for the benefit of such persons,

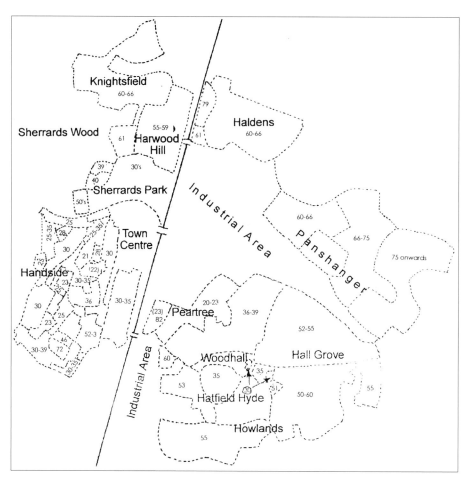

154 The development
of Welwyn Garden City.
The numbers refer to
those years in the 20th
century when
development occurred.

companies and institutions as the company shall
direct'. After six years the fund was to be converted into money. The Trust, the directors of
which were those of the Garden City Company
(with the exception of Reiss), continued with the
same confusing juggling of assets and funds and
made extensive reciprocal use of a subsidiary, the
unrecorded Howardsgate Properties Ltd. It apparently ceased to exist in 1957.

Danesbury Properties Ltd.
Danesbury Properties Ltd., came into existence in
1948. It acquired Lockleys, Tewin Water,
Danesbury and the Lemsford Triangle, land outside the designated area between Brocket Park and
the Great North Road. Chambers and Eccles held
one share each, and the Company 98 shares; the

directors were Chambers, Gray, C.E. Lumb, Eccles
and Major Buckley. It mortgaged, bought, sold
and leased property and transferred shares as freely
as had the old Company, and also bought the
residual leases of property within the town. In
1951 it paid 50 per cent, and in 1952 almost all
its leasehold property was mortgaged, as well as
Lockleys, Danesbury, Guessens and Tewin Water.
In September 1953 Chambers' resignation was not
accepted; it was, however, the following May. In
1953 and 1954 the Trust paid a 40 per cent
dividend.

In December 1953 all the directors of Danesbury
Properties except Eccles tactically resigned. Twenty-
seven thousand five hundred new shares were issued
as well as £32,500 worth of four per cent unsecured
stock. The final payment to the Garden City

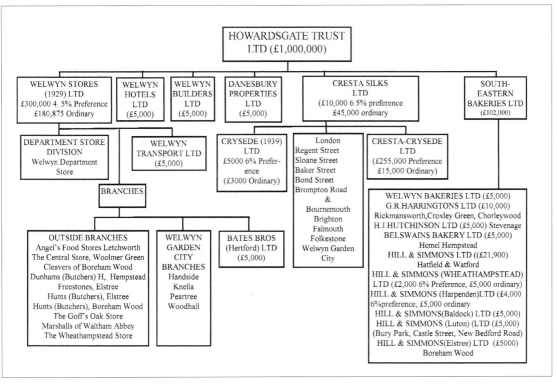

155   The structure of Howardsgate Trust Ltd. around 1950.

shareholders of about 24s. 3d. per share was made by Howardsgate Trust in 1955. In January 1958 Danesbury Estates went into voluntary liquidation and Eccles was appointed administrator. In September 1959, two years after the winding up of the Howardsgate Trust and four years after the final payment to the Garden City's shareholders, the liquidator's accounts were approved and he was instructed to destroy books, accounts and documents within two years. There is no record of the Company's assets or of their disposal.

The Commission for New Towns was set up to take over and manage the property previously vested in the New Towns Corporations. On 1 April 1966 it undertook to operate in Welwyn Garden City until the population should reach a target figure of 40,000. The Corporation ceased to exist after 16 years, by which time the population was about 42,000; there were about 14,000 dwellings, over 100 shops, and four million square feet of factory space.

The Development Corporation exhibited a model of their proposed town centre in 1952, and soon began work on extending existing shops and building new ones in Stonehills. Shops and offices were then developed progressively, filling in the empty spaces. After a long delay the last space, on the corner of Church Road and Parkway, was filled by Sainsbury's in 1982. Several other town centre schemes were put forward under Corporation, Commission and Council only to be either squashed or forgotten. In 1963 the site which the Corporation was most 'anxious to see developed' was the 'Project D', which had contained the first police station. One scheme put forward for this site, in 1968, included an 11-storey tower block.

In 1963 British Rail put forward tentative proposals for redevelopment of the railway station. Similar plans were put forward at intervals for over twenty years. In 1985 the developers, Slough Estates, were concerned that the retail element of

156   The Howard Centre just before it opened in October 1990.

'The Galleria' over the A1(M) at Hatfield would compete with the station scheme. Work stopped on the Howard Centre, 'pending the outcome of the Hatfield public enquiry'. The developers were deliberately misinformed by the District Council, and completed the work in 1990. Subsequently they sued the Council. Rejecting an out-of-court settlement of £16 million, the Council fought the case and lost for £49 million. Eventually a settlement costing £29.75 million was negotiated. No councillors or officers were disciplined and several took early retirement with generous golden handshakes.

Several businesses already in the town moved into the Howard Centre leaving shops empty, and a recent Structure Plan from the Council is concerned with improving the old shopping centre.

External Connections

A factor which was greatly to influence both the development of the Garden City and, more importantly, of the surrounding area, was the construction of highways connecting the New Town to the existing road pattern. At the end of the war, access to the Great North Road was by Valley Road, Stanborough Road or Brockswood Lane. To the east were winding lanes, and to the north development stopped at Coneydale, from the east end of which the Hertford Road was joined at Digswell Water by going down a narrow lane beside the railway (now Harwood Hill), under the viaduct and past Digswell Mill on Digswell Lane (now a cul-de-sac). Fortuitously, a German bomb which fell on the night of 1-2 October 1940 had demolished two houses in Coneydale and cleared the way for a long, straight stretch of Digswell Road to

157 Nos 6 and 8 Coneydale after the bombing in October 1940. Their demolition enabled Digswell Road to be built to the north after the war.

be constructed by the Development Corporation in 1954. Welwyn could then be reached by joining the Great North Road from Knightsfield on the narrow road called, on maps, 'The Avenue' and by locals 'The Row o' Trees'. Re-named Crossway in 1961, it was used by taxi drivers and emergency services until it was cut off by the motorway in 1969.

Black Fan Road was extended in 1966 to join a straightened Birchall Lane at its junction with Cole Green Lane near the level crossing. Construction of Mundells had been begun in 1956, when it was connected to Tewin Road, which went under a railway bridge built originally for the light railway. It was proposed to connect it to the B1000 but the work was not completed until 1969; it was turned into a 'circulatory system' in 1972. As work progressed on the Panshanger development, Herns Lane was closed at its junction with the Hertford Road and re-named Old Herns Lane. A new Herns

Lane was constructed, its junction with the B1000 now a quarter of a mile further east.

Broadwater Road and Bessemer Road were originally constructed to serve the industrial area. In 1955 work began on a northward extension of Bessemer Road to join the B1000, curving between Digswell House and Lake to avoid the bottleneck at Digswell Water. It was not opened completely until 1961; the main problems were obtaining consent and constructing the bridge for the road to pass under the Hertford railway line, which was still being used for goods trains.

By the mid-1920s a policeman had been needed for point duty outside Welwyn church at the junction of the Bedford and Stevenage roads. In 1926 one of the first by-pass roads in the country was constructed to take the Great North Road east of the village. In 1960 this was widened, and a roundabout was constructed at *The Clock*, from which a length of motorway took traffic clear of Knebworth and Stevenage; in 1967 a further stretch of motorway

158   Construction of Welwyn by-pass, 1926.

159   Accident on Welwyn by-pass in December 1965. The volume of traffic by this date is obvious. The entrance to Lockleys and the Mimram bridge is on the right.

was built which took it away from Stanborough. The Stevenage and Stanborough diversions were joined by a final stretch in 1973. The A1 at Hatfield (the Barnet by-pass) became a motorway in 1986.

Traffic Control

When Bessemer road was completed more cross traffic was created at Bridge Road. Originally a policeman was put there on point duty. Traffic lights were tried, as were various experimental layouts using islands and curbs made from tyres, before a revolutionary roundabout ('The Staffordshire Knot') was created. This was eventually replaced – by traffic lights.

In the town, Digswell Road originally ran across the Campus, dividing into a small 'D' to allow traffic to cross Bridge Road to and from Parkway, while the larger 'D' allowed traffic from the north end of the Campus to join Bridge Road east and west. In 1964 the smaller 'D' was removed and the larger one turned into a circulatory system. Guessens Road was stopped off at its north end.

De Soissons' plans had made allowance for private car parking in Parkway and Howardsgate, and the better class of housing had garages, but he was unable to anticipate the almost universal ownership of cars, and the volume – and speed – of traffic which was to come. By 1954 the town centre development posed parking problems, and this became a recurring theme in succeeding Corporation reports. Lay-bys were provided in Stonehills in 1959-60 and Wigmores South was pedestrianised and Church Road car park provided.

In 1968 a design for a multi-storey car park to the east of Stonehills was said to be 'in hand'. In

160 An experimental roundabout at the junction of Bessemer Road and Bridge Road East in May 1971. The old laundry is in the background.

161 An undated though almost certainly pre-war photograph of the Campus seen from Welwyn Stores. The White Bridge is in the distance.

162 The Campus car park under construction in 1963. The Cherry Tree is on the left.

1969 a new car park on the east of the Campus was opened, and 'hardstandings' began to be constructed in residential areas to provide off-street parking. The proposal to put an underground car park beneath the Campus was killed by public and Urban District Council opposition; the Campus was in any case covenanted as a public space.

Agreement on the proposed site for the multi-storey car park was bedevilled by the vague proposals by British Rail to develop the station and by the Corporation's scheme for an 'east perimeter' road alongside the railway, the construction of which was to be followed by pedestrianisation of the town centre. The car park was not built until 1974, beside the end of Hunter's Bridge.

163 Sir Theodore's Way was designed to be a prestigious pedestrian way between the Co-op and the commercial block ('project D') which was never built. The coloured paving slabs have disappeared since this picture was taken in 1959.

164 Welwyn Garden City town centre in the late 1960s. Wigmores South (centre) is pedestrianised and Church Road car park open. The Stores' car park (top right) has not yet been made into a sunken roundabout.

The East Perimeter Road

South of the station much of the land on which the GNR had placed an embargo against development had become allotments by 1939. Land between the station and Bridge Road had been dedicated to parking and to a bus station. The junction of Stonehills and Bridge Road, close to the end of the new dual carriageway on the bridge where the perimeter road must inevitably debouch, had been the cause of major congestion. Traffic lights were considered too 'towny' (the first roundabout in the country was said to have been constructed in Letchworth) and a 'circulatory system' with pedestrian underpasses was decided upon. The Stores' car park was compulsorily purchased and the new roundabout was completed in 1965. 'Project D' was effectively blighted, and it is still an open space today. The pedestrian way

constructed in anticipation on its south side and given the prestigious name 'Sir Theodore's Way' is today a sad strip of concrete ending in a ramp and steps. The town-centre pedestrianisation never took place and the east ramp of the pedestrian underpass was not built because the perimeter road (Osborn Way) now passed under the Howard Centre. At the north end it made two sharp right-angled bends to avoid the multi-storey car park; Stonehills, and the line of the ramp, were blocked.

Limited yellow-line parking was first introduced in 1966, and car park charges were introduced in the town centre in 1969. The multi-storey car park beside the approach to the bridge was not completed until 1974. In the same year, after an injunction brought by the Residents' Association had been rescinded, new roads were constructed across the centre of Parkway, north and south of the fountain, and the old ones blocked to prevent traffic into and out of Howardsgate cutting straight across Parkway.

Council Reorganisation

Local government reorganisation in 1974 merged Welwyn Rural District Council, Welwyn Garden City UDC and Hatfield UDC into Welwyn Hatfield Council. The administrative area covered stretches from Ayot St Lawrence and Woolmer Green to Northaw and North Mymms. The new Council began a £30 million development scheme for Panshanger. The following year housing associations, descendants of the 'public utility societies' of fifty years before, began building. In 1978 the Council took over from the Commission 5,800 rented dwellings, 3,400 reversionary interests, 43 shops, four public houses, a filling station and 16 community buildings. The shopping centres and housing-related assets were not handed over for a further four years. Hertfordshire County Council then became the planning authority for the town. Although it was intended that the Development Corporation should have finished its work first, this was far from the case, especially in respect of the Panshanger development.

Sale of Assets

In 1979 the Commission was instructed by the Thatcher government to dispose of assets in order to raise £100 million. The Commission objected strongly to the government's asset stripping, and pointed out that their work had been designed 'to create a town, not to produce readily-marketable investment'. Eight years later the Chairman wrote, 'I am pleased to report that for the sixth successive year the commission has achieved record sales of industrial, commercial and residential property.' The amount raised that year was £168 million.

Conservation

Initially the character of the Garden City had been jealously guarded by the landlord and by covenants on the use of land (as with the Campus). Houses which were not rented were on leasehold land, the lease usually being for 999 years, later changed to 99 years. Under the Leasehold Reform Act of 1967,

householders could purchase their leases. This became a matter of concern for the New Towns Commission in all the towns for which they were responsible. While it was the planning authority there had been little problem. Later use was made of a Management Scheme which made it possible to retain the necessary powers. This was granted in 1973 in the case of Welwyn Garden City, and only for existing New Towns Commission rented or leasehold estates. Parts of the town were also protected by being declared conservation areas under the Planning Act of 1968.

The New Town

Post-war immigrants were not the enthusiastic do-it-yourself citizens that the early pioneers had been. In 1962 the Council pressed the Corporation to provide amenities for young people. A thousand-signature petition called for roller-skating rinks, a cinema, an indoor swimming pool and a dance-hall. In 1968 the Council proposed a 'cultural centre' at Campus West. It is not clear what research was done on potential users, but a limited response by young people to a questionnaire in the *Welwyn Times* called for a discotheque, dance-hall, ice-rink, ten-pin bowling alley, go-karts, roller-skating (currently fashionable), a gymnasium and a theatre. Welwyn Survey Committee, founded in the 1920s to record the history and natural history of the area, was revived to help design a museum for housing the material and objects which had accumulated over the years. Building began in 1972.

Campus West suffered from public rejection from the outset. The daunting, tall, red-brick structure had nothing in common architecturally with its surroundings. It contained a theatre, restaurant and kitchen, billiards and games rooms, but no bowling alley, skating rink, swimming pool, cinema or museum. With 365 seats, the theatre was too large for amateur productions and too small for professional ones. The wide-open unused spaces encouraged vandalism. In the first year the complex lost £92,000. Managers came and went. It was taken over by caterers, who were sacked; the kitchen and restaurant were closed. Despite a report from a support committee blaming 'bad and confused management, an inferior programme of activities and abysmal publicity', the central tower was turned

into offices for the Council in 1977; cynics concluded that had always been the secret agenda.
Where would the offices have been otherwise?

Parts of the building are only open at certain
times. The lavatories on the ground floor were
bricked up 'because library users (the responsibility
of the County, not the District Council!) were
using them'. The underfloor heating destroyed the
library floor, which had to be replaced, so the library
was closed for four months. Instead of a museum,
a cubic glass hall was provided for commercial
exhibitions, but the doors were not large enough
for this purpose, and there were no users. Although
emininently unsuitable, it was eventually turned into
a roller-skating rink, which is used one evening a
week. In 1985 the accessible parts of the complex
were upgraded at a cost of £750,000. The centre's
refit included a specially woven carpet incorporat-
ing, as a repeating pattern, the 'initial letters of its
name'. Not 'Campus West' but 'West One' – for
fairly obvious reasons.

Today

The buzz words today are 'sustainable development' and the key objectives are incompatible:
increasing the number of houses, preserving the
green belt and reducing the use of the motor car.
Part of the reason for the last of these is the protection of town centres, and the outlining on new
plans of land classified as having retail development
potential in Welwyn Garden City has led to a welcome if misinformed resurgence of interest in the
environment which has been developed here over
the past 80 years.

The inclusion on these plans of the surviving bit
of 'project D' between the Co-op and the sunken
roundabout is a case in point. This, we are told, is
contrary to the original intention of Ebenezer
Howard. Furious letters to the local paper berate
the Council for daring to contemplate the desecra-
tion of a green space which was, not so long ago,
a patch of rough grass with a muddy track across
it (even if it was intended, by the Development
Corporation, as the location for a multi-storey shopping complex). Its connection with Howard is, to
say the least, tenuous. Howard was the man with
the vision, but he was not the genius with the
plans. His vision was implemented (some might say
'hijacked') by real people operating in a capitalist
society. Howard lived in the Garden City, but he
was never the man in charge of it.

History, someone said, stops short of prophesy.
But it doesn't stop short of hope, and it is to be
hoped that all who read this book will see the
town for what it is, warts and all, strive to conserve
what is worthwhile but, also to improve the rest.

Select Bibliography

There are so many books on Ebenezer Howard and Welwyn Garden City written from the point of view of town planning and social engineering it is impossible to include them all and would be invidious to make a choice. Some of the items in the shorter general list below themselves contain useful bibliographies.

Brettall, K.N., *The Story of Tewin*
Busby, Richard, *The Book of Welwyn* (Barracuda, 1976)
Esserin, Angela, *Archive Photographs Series: Welwyn Garden City* (Chalford, 1995)
Filler, Roger, *A History of Welwyn Garden City* (Phillimore, 1986)
Hill, Marion, *Britain in Old Photographs: Welwyn Garden City* (Sutton, 1999)
Hutton, Barbara (ed.), *Hatfield and its People* (Workers Educational Association, 1959-64)
Johnson, W. Branch, *Welwyn Briefly* (1960)
Johnson, W. Branch, *Welwyn By and Large* (1967)
Munby, Lionel, *The Hertfordshire Landscape* (Hodder and Stoughton, 1977)
Page, William (ed.), *Hertfordshire Victoria County History* (Constable, 1908-14)
Richardson, Robert, *The Book of Hatfield* (Barracuda, 1978)
Rook, Tony, *Of Local Interest, a Book of Welwyn Pubs* (1986)
Rook, Tony, *Before the Railway Came. Welwyn 1820-50* (1994)
Rook, Tony, *Welwyn, A Simple History* (1995)
Rook, Tony, *Welwyn Beginning* (3rd edn. 1995)
Rook, Tony, *A History of Hertfordshire* (Phillimore, 2nd edn. 1997)
Soissons, M. de, *Welwyn Garden City* (Publications for Companies, 1988)
Ward, Dora, *Digswell from Domesday to Garden City* (Tony Rook, 2nd edn. 1995)

Index

Abercrombie, 113
Acland, Colonel, 41, 100
Aethelgifu, 18
Agricultural Guild, 75-6, 79
allotments, 2, 56, 123
Anchor Pightle, 55, **55**
Applecroft Road, 77
Ardath Tobacco, 95
Arm and Sword Yard, **32**, 51
assarts, 26
Assembly Rooms, Welwyn, 53, 54, **54**
Atkins, William, 39
Attimore Hall, 23, **24**, 105
Avdel, 95
Ayot Green, 9, 10, 35, **36**, 109
Ayot St Lawrence, 67, 69
Ayot St Peter, 21, **21**, 39, 56, 67, 69

Backhouse, Edward, 107
Backhouse Rooms, 23, 97, 98, 103, 107
Barn Theatre, 23, 62, 109
Bassingburn family, 46
Bathurst, Rev. Thomas, 48
Baynard, Ralph, 21
Bec, Geoffrey de, 23
Belgae, 13, **13**, 18, 53, **53**
Bessemer Road, 39, 92, 95, 119-20
Bills, Elizabeth, 1
Black Death, 51
Black Fan, **8**, 53, 59
blacksmiths, 51
Blake family, 48, 54, 60
Boteler family, 46
boulder clay, 6, 25-6
Bournville, 2
bowls, 53, 105, 106
Brewery Hill, 64

brick(works), 10-11, 78, 82, **83**
Brickwall Hill (Farm), 14, 23, 75, **76**
Bridge Road, **23**, 62, 85, 120
Broadwater Road, 79, 94-5, **94**, 119
Brocket (Durants Hyde), 5, 26, 35, **41**, 42, 53, 101
Brocket, Edward, 47
Brockswood Lane, 85, 118
Bronze Age, 12-13, **12**
Broomfield, 31
Buckley, Major, 116
building societies, 2
Bulls Green, 10
Burghley, Robert Cecil, 44
bus services, 87
Bush Hall, 58

Campus, the, 69, **81**, 82, **83**, 101, 102, 107, 109, 120, **121**, 122, **122**
Campus West, 109, 124-5
Carnegie Chemicals, 102
Carrington, J., 61
Carter, Francis, 44
Cathcart, Lady, 43, 57
Cavendish, William, 44
Cecil family, 11, 23, 33, 46. *See also* Burghley *and* Salisbury
cemeteries, 14-15, 18, **19**, 58
chalk, 6-7, 9, 12-13
Chamber of Commerce, 95
Chambers, Sir Theodore, 71-2, **72**, 80, 91, 115, 116
Chequers, **107**
Chequers, the (brewhouse), 49-50, **50**
churches:
    Anglican Mission chapel, Harmer Green, 64
    Baptist, 62, **63**, 103

Bethel Independent, 62
Catholic, 62, 103
Christian Scientist, 103
Christian Spiritualist, 103
Congregationalist, 103
Evangelical, 62
Free Church, 103
Independent, 56-7
Methodist, 64
'Moo-cow Chapel', 62
Pentecostal Assembly, 64
Quaker, 103
St Etheldreda's (Audrey's), Hatfield, 20
St Francis, 102, 103
St John's, Digswell, 21, 103
St John's, Lemsford, 21
St Mary Magdalene, Hatfield Hyde, **63**, 64, 103
St Mary the Virgin, Welwyn, 18, **19**, **20**, 35
St Michael's Hall, 103
St Peter's, Tewin, 20
Synagogue, 103
Wesleyan, 62
Church House, Welwyn, 9, 52, 61
Church Street, Welwyn, 16
cinema, 69, 109, **109**
Clavering family, 38-9
coaching, 35, 64, 67
Cobble End, 37, **66**
Codicote, 16, 49, 59
Cole Green House, 38-9
Commission for New Towns, 117, 124
Coneydale, 118, **119**
Co-operative societies, 2, 88, 90
County Council (Herts), 61-2, 64, 100, 124
Cowper, Earl, 11, 38-9, 42, 43, 44, 48, 54, 57, 60
Cresta Silks, 91, 115
cricket, 54, 106
Crickmer, C.M., 82, 84
Crookhams, 13
Croydon Moldright Co., 95
Cuyler, General, 48, 53

Dacre, Lord, 66
Daily Mail, 82
Danesbury, 28, 31, 48, 61, **61**, 100, 110, 116
Danesbury Properties Ltd., 116-17
Daniells, 13

Datchworth Green, 15
Dawley Wood, 12
Dering, George (Mr. Dale), 41, 61
Desborough, Lord, 4, 26, 39, 71
Development Corporation(s), 72, 85, 95, 101, 113-15, 117, 119, 124
Dewar, Michael, 48, 100
Dicket Mead, 15, 57, **57**
Digswell (village), 18, 21, 25, 37, 49, 59, 67
Digswell House, 4, 11, 23, 39-41, **40**, 44, 48, 51, 119
Digswell Lodge, 23, **24**
Digswell Survey, 25, **25**, 39, **39**, 48, 53, **87**
Digswell Viaduct, 66, **66**
Digswell Water, 9, 12, 39, **40**, 82, 118, 119
doctors, 58, 100-1
Dogen Hyde, 26
Domesday Book, 17, **17**, 21-3, 25
drains, 58-9
drove roads, 34

Eccles, J.F., 80, 90, 115-17
Educational Association, 97, 109
Elizabeth I, 34, 44
Ellesfield, 16
Elm Gardens, 77
Ely, Abbots of, 17, 20, 21, 25, 44, 47
Ermine Street, 15

Faithful, Rev. F.J., 37, 57
fields, 25
film studios, 95, **95**
fire-fighting, 60, 61-2, 62
First Garden City Ltd., 2-3
Fleet, James, 43
flint, 9, 12, 13
football, 54, 105-6
Fore Street, 10-11, 35
fossils, **7**
Freeman, Rev. Ralph, 48
Freemantle, Colonel, 80
Fretherne House, 98, 101
Friendly Societies, 2, 54
Frythe, The, 26, 28, 47, 95, 96

Garden City and Town Planning Association, 2-4
Garden City Pioneer Company, 2

gasworks, 60-1
Gernon, Robert, 21
Gill Hill, 16
GlaxoSmithKline, 47, 96-7
Goldings, 51
golf, 42, 54
Gosling, R. (Stadium), 106, **107**
'gout track', the, 64
Grange, The, 10, 14, 18
gravels, 6-7, 13, 82, **84**
Gray, L., 115, 116
Great North Road, 5, 11, 23, 34-7, **65**, 67, **76**, 85, 118
Groves, John, 43
Grubs Barn, 18, 53
Guessens, 11, 48, 95, 109, 116
Guessens Road, 79
Guild of Health, 101
'gum-boot era', 87

Haldens, 103, 114
Hampstead Garden Suburb, 82
Handside, 26, 47, 85, 106
Handside Lane, 82
Handside Nurseries, 80
Hatfield, 4, 5, 16-17, 18, 21, 23, 25, 33, 33-4, 35, 37, 48, 51, 53, 61-2, 87, 110
Hatfield Great Hall, 11
Hatfield House, 10, **22**, 33, 35, 44, **44**, 46
Hatfield (West) Hyde, 18, 26, **27**, **28**, 46
Hatfield market house, **22**, 23, 57
Hatfield Newtown ('California'), **31**, 33
Hatfield Palace, 10, **22**, 34, 44, **45**
Havilland, de, 34, 97
Hawbush, 31
Health Association (Council), 98, 101
Herns Lane, 119
Hertford Road, 16, 39, 41, 43, 48, 58, 118
Hertingfordbury (vill), 21
High Oaks Road, 82
hockey, 105-6
Hollies, The, 101
Holwell (Hyde), 26, 39, 46
Horn, W.J., W.C., 28, 75
Horn's sidings, 69, 82
hospitals, 59-60, 100-1
    Cottage Hospital, 98, 101, 105
    New Danesbury, 100

    Queen Elizabeth II Hospital, 101, **101**
    Queen Victoria Hospital, 59-60, **60**, 100
housing, 77-9, **78**, 81, 85, 91, 110
Howard, Ebenezer, 1-5, 39, 41, 71, 81, 84, 107, 110, 113, 125; *Tomorrow*, 1-2, **1**
Howard Centre, 69, 117-18, **118**, 123
Howard Cottage Society, 3
Howardsgate, 89, **90**, 90-1, 107, 121
Howardsgate (Investment) Trust, 72, 114-17, **117**
Howardsgate Properties Ltd., 116
Hughes, W.R., 72
Hunter's Bridge, 85, 87, 92, 122
hunting, 53
Hutchinson, Rev. Julius, 46

ICI, 42, 46, 95
Industrial Transfer Scheme, 95
Ingles, 114

James I, 44, 53
James, Captain, 82
Justices of the Peace, 51

Kerr, Admiral Walter, 42
Knebworth, 59, 119
Knightsfield, 11, 85, 119

Lamb family, 39, 42
land-fill sites, 69, 106
Lanes, 5, 48, 85-7, **87**
Lawrence Hall, 97, 101, 103, 107, **108**, 109
Lea river, 4, 6, 15, 26, 49, 58-9
Leasehold Reform Act (1967), 124
Lemmens, Major, 89
Lemsford, 15, 18, 35, 49, 58, 109, 116
Letchworth, 2-3, 82, 105, 123
libraries, 54-5, 56, 109
Lincoln Electric, 95-6, **96**
Lizard Lane, 35
Lockleys, 10, 13, 16, 23, 28, 39, **41**, 48, 68, 95, 98, 110, 116
Longcroft Lane, 11, 79
Looking Backward, 1
Lower Handside, 23, 28, 75, 79
Luda, Roger de, William de, 46
Ludwick Hall, 9, 23, 39, 46, **46**
Ludwick Hyde, 26, 46, 51

Ludwick Way, 79
Lumb, C.E., 116
Lunardi, Vincent, 97
Luton, 69, 70
Lyle's Bridge, 85
Lyminge, Robert, 44
Lytton, Lord, 100

McGuire, Hugh, 43
malt-making, 49-51
Mandeville: Geoffrey de, 22; William de (Earl of Essex), 39
Manor House, Welwyn, 14, 28, 48, 51
Marden, 43-4
Mardley Hill, 37
match manufacturers, 92
Meadow Green, 82
Melbourne, Viscount, 39, 42
Mill Green, 6, 15, 49, 59
Mill Lane, 11, 31
mills, *see also* watermills, 10, 23
Mimram river, 4, 6, 15, 39, 49, 113
monasterium, 15, 18
Montford, Thomas, 42
motorways, 59, 109, 120
Mountain Slough, 16, 35, 64, **64**
Mundells, 119
Murphy, Frank, 94

Nall-Cain, Charles, 42
National Garden Cities Committee, 3
Neale, Mrs. Rosa, Richard, 41-2
New Town Builders Ltd., 79
New Towns Act (1946), 113
New Towns Trust (Welwyn Pioneer Trust), 23, 72-3, 75-6, 79, 81, 97, 101
Normans, 9, 17
Norton Abrasives, 95

Old Rectory, Welwyn, 8-9, 31, 48
Osborn, Frederic, 3, 4, 71-2, **72**, 84
Osborn Way, 123
Otway family, 54, 55

Page, F.M., 80
Paine, Thomas, 42
Palmerston, Lord, 39, 42
Panshanger, 2, 4, 5, 8, 38-9, **38**, 48, 103, 110,

114, 124
Panshanger flying school, 8, 97
Parkway, **77**, 84-5, 121
Peartree, 28, 89, **100**, 101
Peat, Sir Harry, 79
Pentley Close, 14
Perient family, 39
Pilot, the, 76-7
Poleyn, John, Anne, 47
police force, 51, **52**
Polycel, 95
Polypenco, 96
Port Sunlight, 2
Prospect Place, 13, 61
Pryor Reid and Co., 50, **50**
public houses:
    Beehive, the, 23, 105
    Boars Head, The, 35
    Bull, the, 37
    Cherry Tree, the, **104**, 105, 107, **122**
    Clock, The, 37
    Doctor's Tonic, the, 105
    Fairway Tavern, the, 105
    Fountain, the, 105
    Green Man, the, **104**, 105
    Hedgehog, the, 105
    Hollybush, the, 105, **114**
    Long Arm and Short Arm, the, 62, 103
    Mayflower, the, 105
    North Star, the, 37, 56
    Oak Tavern, the, 105
    Railway Tavern, the (*Cowper Arms Hotel*), 37
    Red Lion, the (*Leg o'Mutton*), 23, 35, **51**, 103
    Rose and Crown, the, 35
    Salisbury Arms, the (*Gate House*), 10, **10**, 37, 53
    Salisbury Temperance Hotel, the, **36**, 37
    Sun, The, 103
    Swan, The, 35, 54
    Vine, The, 54
    Waggoners, The, 103
    Wellington, The, 9, 35
    White Hart, the, 10, 35, 53, 54
    Woodman, the (*Chieftain*), 105
Public Loans Commission, 77
Public Utility Societies, 79, 81
Purdom, C.B., 3, 4, 71, 79-80, 88-9, 103; *The Garden City*, 3

Queen Hoo, 10
Queensway, 31

railways, 5, 11, 37, 64-70, **66**, **68**, **69**, **70**, 82, 84-5, **84**, **85**, 91
Rectory, Welwyn, 23, 31
Reddings, 113
Reiss, Richard L., 3, 71, 79, 81, 101, 103, 113, 115-16; *The Home I Want*, 3
Repton, Humphry, 39, 43, **43**
Residents Associations, 51
Robbery Bottom, 15
Roche Products, 96
Romans, 5, 9-10, **9**, 13-15, 18, 53
Rose Green, 58
Rowntree Village Trust, 3
rugby, 105-6
Russells, 101

Sabine, Joseph, 42-3, **42**
St Albans, 6, 15, 43, 53, 69-70, 87
St Bartholomew's, Smithfield, 38, 42
St John Lodge, Danesbury, 48
St Mary's Hall, 54-5
St Michael, Lawrence de, 39
Salisbury, Lord, 4, 26, 44, 46, 57, 58, 67-8, 71, 110
Salisbury Square, **32**, 33
Sault, J.W., 76-7, 80
Savill, Norman, 4, 71
Saxons, 6, 15, 18, 25, 51
School Lane, 15, 16, 59
School Lane brewery, 49, **50**
schools:
    Attimore (Sir Frederic Osborn), 99
    Catholic, 98, 99
    early schools (Ayot St Peter, Digswell, Hatfield, Hatfield Hyde, Lemsford, Tewin) 57; (Welwyn) 55-7; (Garden City) 98-100
    Grammar (Stanborough), 14, 98-9, **99**
    Heronswood, 99, **99**
    Howard Secondary Modern (Sir John Newsome), 99
    Monks Walk, 56, 99
    National Schools, 55-7
    St Margaret's, 42
    Sherrardswood, 42, 98, **98**
Searle, Edward, 41

Second Garden City Company Ltd., 69, 71
Sefton, Malcolm, 113
Selfridges, 88
sewage farm, 58-9, **59**
Sewells Orchard, 12
Shallcross family, 39, 46
Shaw, G.B., 5, 69
Shee, George, 41, 54
Sherrardspark (Wood), 5, 6, 7, 11, 12, 39, 110-13
Shoplands, 103, 114
shops, 89, 90-1, 114
Shredded Wheat, 92-4, **93**
Silkin, Lewis, 113
Skinner, J., 113
Soane, Sir John, 44
Soissons, Louis de, 77, 82-4, 85, **86**, 91
Speight, F.W., 11
Springfields Road, 110
Stanborough (Farm), **29**, **75**, 80
Stanborough Estates Ltd., 80-1
steel manufacture, 92, **93**
street lighting, 60-1
Stone Age, 12, **12**
Stonehills ('Project D'), 53, 89, 117, 121, **122**, 123, 125
'swallow holes', 6-8, **8**, 106
swimming, **105**, 106, **106**

Taylor, W.G., 3
tennis, 54
Tewin, 5, 15, 17, 18, 21, 25, 39, 42-3, 49, 100
Tewin Water, 11, 43, **43**, **47**, 48, 110, 116
Thames river, 6
Thorkell, 21
Tigwell, H.T., 113
timber-framing, 8-9, 11
Tinkers Hill, 80, 89
Tithe Apportionment Act, 25, **26**, **64**, 87
Tova (Marden), 43
trades unions, 2, 75
turnpikes, 35, **35**, 60, 64
Twentieth Mile Bridge, 11, 46, 70, 85

Underwood, 80, 89
Upper Handside, 23, 28, 107, 109

Valognes: Agnes de, 41; Christiana de, 39; Gunnora de, 18, 47; Peter de, 20, 21

Van Gogh, Vincent, 56
Victoria, Queen, 39, 42
Vineyard, The, 11
Vineyard Barn, 23, **24**

Water End, 15
watermills, 15, 49
Watling Street, 15
Watton at Stone, 15
Wellfield Road, 33, 61
Welwyn (village), 5, 17, 18, 21-3, 28-31, **29**,
    30, **31**, 35, 39, 49, 58, 59, 61, 110
Welwyn Brickworks Ltd., 73
Welwyn Builders and Joiners Ltd., 73, 77, 115
Welwyn by-pass, **4**, 31, 119, **120**
Welwyn Dairies Ltd., 76
Welwyn Electrical Installations Ltd., 115
Welwyn Garden City Company, 28, 72-3, 76,
    79-81, 82, 87, 88, 89, 90, 91, 97-8, 101,
    105, 110-16; shareholders, 73, 77, 81, 114-
    17
Welwyn Garden City Urban District Council,
    28, 59, 62, 77, 87, 98, 106, 113, 118
Welwyn Hatfield Council, 124, 125

Welwyn Nurseries Ltd., 73
Welwyn Publications Ltd., 76-7, 113
Welwyn Restaurants Ltd., 80, 105
Welwyn Rural District Council, 31, 61, 67, 77
Welwyn Stores Ltd., 73, 75, 77, 80, 88-9, **88**,
    89, 90-1, **91**, 101, 109, 115
Welwyn Theatres Ltd., 73
Welwyn Times, the, 77, **111**, 124
Welwyn Transport Ltd., 73, 115
Welwyn tunnel, 70, **70**
Wheathampstead, 15, 100
White Bridge, 85, 100
Wigmores South, 89, 121
Wilshere family, 47, 54, 100
Wilshere Road, 31
Wingfield, Rev. Charles, 48
Wood, Joseph, 42
Woodhall (Hatfield), 26, **45**, 46, 53, 75, 90
Woodland Rise, 113
Woolmer Green, 35
Wrestlers' Bridge, **33**, 34

Young, Dr. Edward, 48, 54, 55
youth clubs, 54, 107